CHINA!
CHRISTIAN MARTYRS
OF THE
20th CENTURY

an excerpt from
BY THEIR BLOOD

by
James and Marti Hefley

mott media
Box 236 Milford MI 48042

Copyright © 1978 by James C. Hefley

All rights reserved

No part of this book may be reproduced or transmitted in any form or by any means, electronic or mechanical, including photocopying, recording, storage in any information retrieval system, or other, without written permission of the publisher. Brief quotations embodied in critical articles or reviews are permitted.

Printed in the United States of America

ISBN 0-915134-16-0

Library of Congress No. 78-6187

PREFACE

Christian martyrs! The words stir the imagination. A saint singing above flames that crackle around his stake. A believer kneeling serenely before a blood-stained block; the gimlet-eyed executioner preparing to swing his sword. A missionary bound with vines beside a bubbling pot, his eyes lifted confidently to heaven, while loin-clothed cannibal aborigines dance wildly around to the beat of booming drums.

But burning at the stake passed out of style after Reformation times. Death by the sword rarely occurs today. And only a few missionaries have ever been cooked by cannibals. Such macabre martyrdoms more often occur in the imagination of novelists.

Martyrs of the 20th century have met their earthly end in more conventional, up-to-date methods such as gunshots, bombs, banditry, debilitating prison diseases and starvation.

A second oversimplification is that Christian martyrs always die strictly for their testimony of Christ. This idea persists because accounts of martyrdom often do not include sufficient backgrounding of the events. When all the details are known, it is apparent that most Christian martyrs die in circumstances *related* to their witness for Christ. For example, five young American missionaries were speared to death in 1956 by Auca Indians in Ecuador because of the Indians' fear that they were cannibals. And nurse Mavis Pate was killed by gunfire from a Palestinian refugee camp because Arab commandos mistook the Volkswagen Microbus in which she was riding for an Israeli army vehicle. However, some Christians are killed *primarily* for their allegiance to Christ. Most martyrs to communism in China and the Soviet Union fit into this category.

So the first dictionary definition of martyr—"One who submits to death rather than renounce his religion"—cannot always be strictly applied to the violent death of Christians. The second definition—"One who dies, suffers, or sacrifices everything for a principle, cause, etc."—is more inclusive. By this delineation Lottie Moon, the heroine of Southern Baptists, who died from self-imposed starvation in China was as much a martyr as John and Betty Stam, who were brutally murdered by cold, calculating Chinese Communists.

Recognizing this, we have included many martyrs who might be excluded in some books because they did not die a violent death. At the same time we have not classified as martyrs those who died in accidents which might have happened to them in the homeland. Admittedly, the line is hard to draw here.

We have sought to provide stories of the deaths of Christian nationals where reliable information is available. This is often not the case. Young churches, developing amidst persecution, are less likely to keep records than established congregations with more time and freedom. National believers, also, because of educational and communicational disadvantages, do not document and preserve the stories of their own who have died for Christ. These stories are usually transmitted orally and later written down by educated leaders and/or missionaries. In contrast, the stories of most missionary martyrs and nationals who die with them are well attested. Books by eyewitnesses or close relatives have even been written about some of them.

We have generally restricted our time limit to the 20th century, although in giving background and introducing the martyrs of a country or area, we have usually summarized hostilities to Christianity before the year 1900. In instances of both martyred nationals and missionaries, we have also sought to understand the political, national and social forces behind great outbreaks, such as the Boxer Rebellion of China and the more recent Congo massacre.

After all the circumstances have been considered, we recognize that every martyr died for a purpose within the sovereign will of God. God was there when every human life was taken—not setting up the deaths, but permitting evil men to exercise their free will and to do their dastardly deeds under the temporary dominion of Satan. But he was there in grace abounding over sin, beauty growing out of ashes, victory triumphing over death, and the church advancing beyond defeat.

With this introduction, we now present the China section of *By Their Blood: Christian Martyrs of the 20th Century*. This is a sampling of the larger book to follow, which represents the largest research project we have undertaken during the past decade. A complete bibliography will be included in the larger book.

James and Marti Hefley
Signal Mountain, Tennessee

Editor's Note: *The Standard Wade—Giles System of Romanization, but without the diacritical marks, as presented in Mathews'* Chinese-English Dictionary, *Revised American Edition (Cambridge: Harvard University Press, 1963), has been used for place names, except those commonly known cities which are given the spellings used by the Postal System. Personal names have followed either the common Romanization of names or a more Westernized form when preferred by the person. The names of some towns and cities have been changed under the Communist Chinese regime; we are using the older form, as used at the time of the event.*

MARTYRS OF CHINA

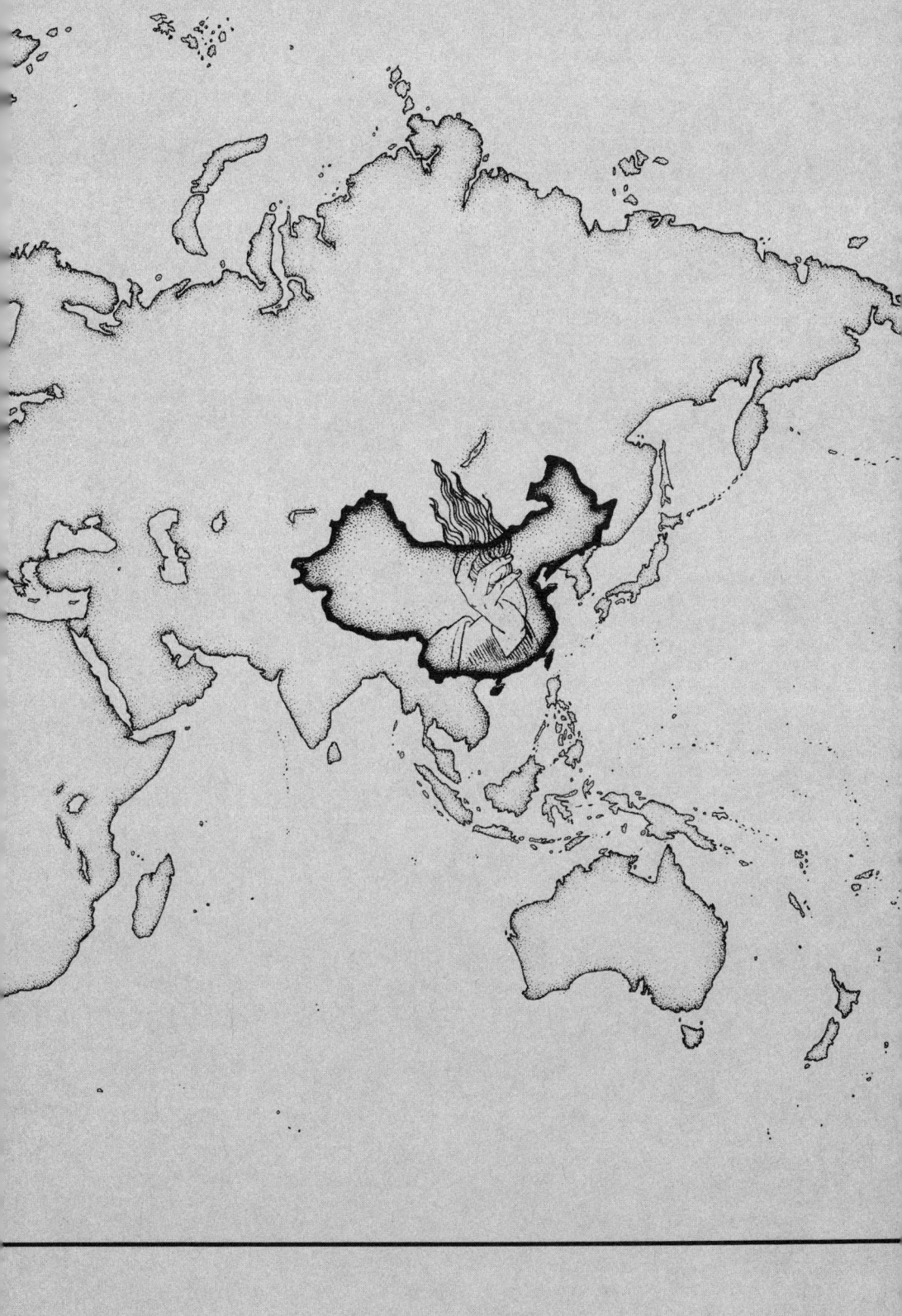

THE FURY OF THE BOXERS:
China, 1900

BY IMPERIAL COMMAND EXTERMINATE THE CHRISTIAN RELIGION! DEATH TO THE FOREIGN DEVILS! In June, 1900, crazed mobs bannered this terrible proclamation as they rampaged through cities of north China, looting and burning churches and the homes of missionaries and Chinese Christians. They were led by bare-chested fanatics called Boxers who brandished long-curving swords and cried for the heads and hearts of Christians and missionaries.

Item: In Manchuria, where all missionaries managed to escape, a Chinese pastor was caught. When he refused to deny Christ, his eyebrows, ears and lips were cut off. Still he would not recant. His heart was then cut out and put on display in a theater. His fourteen-year-old daughter, following the example of her father, suffered a like fate.

Item: In Shansi Province Mary Huston and Hattie Rice, two young single women affiliated with the China Inland Mission, strove to flee an angry mob. Miss Rice was beaten to death by the roadside. Miss Huston, seriously injured by a cart run over her to break her spine, died a month later.

Item: At remote Tsun-hua the Chinese Methodist pastor was forced to a pagan temple, mocked before idols, then left tied to a pillar. He spent the night preaching while friends pleaded with him to recant. In the morning a thousand-strong mob descended on him and literally tore out his heart. Two Chinese women teachers who were captured, also refused to renounce Christianity. The feet of one were chopped off and she was then killed with a sword. The other—shouting to her pupils, "Keep the faith!"—was wrapped in cotton, soaked with kerosene and burned alive. One hundred sixty-three Chinese Methodists in Tsun-hua were martyrs for Christ in June, 1900. Only four or five escaped.

As the blood flowed, newspaper headlines abroad screamed:

    CHINESE MASSACRE MISSIONARIES

and a shocked world asked why.

Intrigue Leads to Tragedy

The world's most populous nation had appeared to be moving from idolatrous darkness toward the light of Christianity. Converts had been doubling and redoubling in recent years, circulation of Scripture running in the millions. The China Inland Mission (CIM; now Overseas Missionary Fellowship), largest of the evangelical agencies in China, had welcomed over a thousand new workers in the past decade. Other missions were also expanding, but on a lesser scale.

Western churches spoke of China as "our largest and most promising mission field." Yet ironically, Christianity had reached China centuries before Columbus sighted America. In fact, an eighth century Chinese Nestorian church leader claimed the Magi, returning from Bethlehem, had brought the first news of the Savior.

Christianity had waxed and waned until around 1300 when Franciscans arrived and tried to dominate the Chinese church. Their actions provoked intervention by Asian Moslems who had been abiding by a truce. The aroused Moslems killed hundreds of thousands of Christians, piling seventy thousand heads on the ruins of one city. Organized Christianity was swept from Asia.

The Jesuit order came in the sixteenth century and in 1705 convinced the Chinese emperor to make China a Catholic state. A sharp rebuff came from the pope who said the emperor could not be a Christian and continue to worship his ancestors. In 1724 Christianity was banned, and hundreds of Catholic missionaries and converts were put to death.

The first Protestant missionary, Robert Morrison, went out as an employee of the East India Company in 1807. He translated almost the entire Bible into the main Chinese language, but when he died in 1834 there were only three known Chinese Christians in the whole Empire.

Western military and political pressure opened the door for the entrance of foreign missionaries in the latter half of the nineteenth century. Hundreds poured in and took up stations across the vast mysterious land.

Disease, travel accidents and violence took a heavy toll. The average life expectancy dropped to forty. The countryside rumbled with frequent rebellions against the central Manchu government in Peking. Missionaries were often caught between opposing forces, and some gave their lives. For example, an early Southern Baptist worker, J. Landrum Holmes, and an Episcopal missionary were killed while trying to intercede with rebels for the safety of their town.

Added to the rebellions was the continuing encroachment of foreign powers. By 1898 the political situation was so chaotic that young Emperor Kuang-hsu decided Christian moral and social reforms were the only hope for saving China from total foreign domination. He asked Timothy Richard, an influential British Baptist missionary, to come to the palace to help draw up the reforms. But on the very day Richard arrived, the emperor was deposed in a coup by underlings controlled by the secret Boxer Society, who feared the emperor was about to sell out the nation.

The Righteous Ones, as the Boxers were called, bitterly opposed Christianity, which they termed "the religion of the foreign devils." In a desperate effort to preserve the old pagan religions, they had established a network of secret cells across China. Initiates repeated a sacred formula until they fell foaming at the mouth, then joined in a black magic ritual that sometimes included human sacrifices to temple idols. The Boxers claimed they were commanded by "heavenly deities," and were thus invulnerable. A potion smeared on them by their priests was supposed to make them bulletproof.

Following the coup, the Boxers and their supporters installed the emperor's mentally ill aunt, Tzu Hsi, on the throne. They persuaded the empress that missionaries were stealing Chinese spirits and gouging out the eyes of Chinese children for use in their medicines. At their urging, she issued a secret order to officials in the provinces calling for the execution of all foreigners. As the nineteenth century faded, Boxer organizers fanned out across China, recruiting new members, preparing to strike when the empress delivered her edict. They moved cautiously, knowing that the great majority of local officials were opposed to violence and determined to keep law and order.

Sometimes fanatical zeal overtook strategy. In Shantung Province, for example, they captured a young English missionary, Sidney Brooks, returning from vacation on December 30, 1899. After torturing him for hours, they killed him. At his murder the foreign community demanded punishment. Two Boxers were executed for the crime and Governor Yu-hsien, a Boxer supporter, was replaced.

Throughout the spring of 1900 the fanatical Boxers agitated the populace by stirring up historic Chinese racial pride in their nation as the celestial center of the world. They fired hatred against foreign powers for forcing exploitative treaties on the country and sustaining the hated opium trade which kept millions of Chinese addicted. They fueled resentment over jobs lost through foreign building of railroads. In northern China, which had suffered crop failures for three years, the Boxers blamed missionaries and their foreign religion for the long drought. "The foreigners have insulted our gods," they declared. "Foreign blood must be spilled before our gods will send rain." The Boxers also capitalized on enmity which had developed against Catholic missionaries when the French government had actually forced the Chinese government to give Catholic prelates power equal to judges and magistrates.

Still the foreigners did not become alarmed until it was too late for many to flee. After all, many reasoned, China had always seethed with rebellions and banditry, and even so the CIM had lost only one missionary to mob violence, although other martyrdoms had occurred. Danger went with the work, the missionaries assumed, and went on about their business of preaching, teaching and healing.

The Terror Begins

In March the empress appointed the notorious, known Boxer supporter Yu-hsien governor of Shansi, the northern province where much missionary work was concentrated. In June the German and Japanese ambassadors were murdered in Peking.

The alarmed foreign community grouped in the British embassy compound and began building fortifications as Boxers paraded through the Imperial capital.

The royal edict to kill all foreigners and exterminate Christianity was given to couriers for delivery to provincial governors. Messengers to the south, however, changed one Chinese character on the decree, so that it read "protect" instead of "kill" foreigners. For this disobedience they were cut in half. But the missionaries and Christians in this area were saved, and the bloodletting was confined to the northern provinces.

One hundred eighty-eight foreign missionaries and missionary children were murdered during the Boxer wrath in the summer of 1900, all in four provinces. Most of these casualties were suffered in Shansi Province under the diabolical governor Yu-hsein. Of the 159 foreigners who died in Shansi Province, 91 were associated with the China Inland Mission.

Rugged Shansi Province is the cradle of ancient Chinese civilization. The famous Emperor Yao lived and ruled from here over the "black-haired race" eight hundred years before Abraham was born. Shansi is an inhospitable land, bitterly cold in winter and fiercely hot in summer. Topographically, it is mostly high undulating tablelands, punctuated by steep hills and sandwiched between the Yellow River on the west and a rugged mountain range on the east. Shansi was not an easy place from which foreigners could escape.

The Governor's Treachery

The bloodiest massacre took place in the ancient Shansi provincial capital Taiyuan where the gates of the walled city were closed to prevent the foreigners from escaping. Trapped in their residences were twenty-four adults and nine children, associated with the Baptist Missionary Society of England, the CIM, and the small Sheo Yang Mission which operated the Schofield Memorial Hospital in a satellite town.

The doctor for whom the hospital was named had died of typhus fever in 1883, contracted from a patient admitted by the gatekeeper without the doctor's knowledge. Shortly before his death, he had begged for reinforcements. Two medics had answered his call, Dr. Willaim M. Wilson and Dr. E.H. Edwards. Dr. Edwards took charge of the Schofield Hospital. Dr. Wilson, who was with the CIM, operated a hospital for opium addicts in an outlying city at his own expense. To these doctors thousands of persons owed their lives.

Dr. Edwards was safely away when the crisis came. Dr. Wilson and his wife and young son were due for furlough, but had stayed on to help during the famine. Early in the summer Mrs. Wilson and son went ahead to Taiyuan for rest from the baking heat. The doctor remained to care for his patients until he fell prey to peritonitis. One of his last acts of mercy was to travel twenty dangerous miles to save the life of Pastor Si who lay severely wounded from a Boxer sword slash in his side. Before the doctor left for treatment in Taiyuan, Chinese Christians presented him with a large red satin sash, bearing the gilt inscription "God's Faithful Servant." His last letter was written on the road to Taiyuan. "It's all fog," he wrote a colleague, "but I think, old chap, that we are on the edge of a volcano, and I fear Taiyuan is the inner edge."

Besides Mrs. Wilson, two CIM single women missionaries were in Taiyuan. Jane Stevens, a nurse, was in frail health. During her last trip back to England for rest, a friend had suggested that a position in the homeland might be easier. Nurse Stevens had replied, "I don't feel I have yet finished the work God has for me in China. I must go back. Perhaps—who knows?—I may be among those allowed to give their lives for the people."

Miss Stevens had come to China in 1885. Her Taiyuan partner, Mildred Clarke, came in 1893. Upon reaching Taiyuan, Miss Clarke wrote home, "I long to live a poured-out life unto Him among these Chinese, and to enter into the fellowship of His sufferings for souls, who poured out His life unto death for us."

Of the other missionaries at Taiyuan nine were former CIM members: six had joined the small Sheo Yang Mission which operated the Schofield Memorial Hospital; W.T. and Emily Beynon were now representatives of the British and Foreign Bible Society; Alexander Hoddle was independent, operating a small Christian bookstore and teaching English to Chinese students for his support.

At the Sheo Yang Mission were T.W. and Jessie Pigott and their young son Wellesley. A friend had written of Mr. Pigott, "If ever a man lived in earnest, it was Thomas Wellesley Pigott." A man of many talents, he could fix anything. Emily Pigott, though not a doctor, was skilled at removing eye cataracts. Old China hands, the Pigotts had lost friends in an earlier massacre—four Church Missionary Society workers killed by the radical vegetarian sect in Fukien Province in 1895. Since then the Piggots had felt their time would be short in China and had worked almost nonstop. Another prophetic note had been sounded by W.T. Beynon in the ending of his 1899 report to the Bible Society: "We trust that this coming year the God of all grace will give all of us grace to be faithful."

Violence exploded in late June, 1900. Mobs roamed the streets, setting fire to the compounds of the British Baptists and the Sheo Yang group. The missionaries and a group of Chinese believers linked hands and sought refuge in the Baptist boys' school about a half mile away. After reaching the school, Edith Coombs of the Sheo Yang Mission suddenly realized she had left two Chinese schoolgirls behind, one of whom was very sick. Miss Coombs broke away and ran back to the blazing buildings to rescue them. As they were rushing out, the sick girl stumbled and fell. Miss Coombs bent to lift her and shield her from the brickbats being hurled by the mob. The mob moved in closer, forced them to separate, and drove the missionary back into the house. The mob and the Chinese girls she had tried to rescue last saw her kneeling in the flames.

The remaining thirty-two missionaries and children, along with their loyal Chinese friends, barricaded themselves in the boys' school. Day and night stones pelted the walls and doors while the group inside waited and prayed behind barricades, hoping for rescue by the provincial governor, Yu-hsien, whose palace was a short distance away.

On July 9 soldiers arrived and escorted the missionaries to the courtyard of the governor's palace where they joined twelve Catholic clergy. The missionaries, thinking they would now be saved, saw they were doomed when Yu-hsien stormed out waving his sword and shouting, "Kill! Kill!"

The governor announced that the men would die first. George Farthing, one of the English Baptists and the father of three children, stepped forward. His wife clung to him, but he gently put her aside and knelt before the chopping block without a murmur. His head fell with one stroke of the executioner's sword.

The other men were killed one by one, then the women and children. The Farthing children hung on to their mother and had to be pulled away when she was ordered to kneel. Mrs. Lovitt was permitted to hold the hand of her little boy. "We all came to China to bring you the good news of salvation by Jesus Christ," she said in a firm voice. "We have done you no harm, only good. Why do you treat us so?" In a strange act of gentleness, a soldier stepped up and removed her spectacles before she and her son were beheaded.

The priests and nuns died with equal courage. Their bishop, an old man with a white beard, asked the governor, "Why are you doing this wicked deed?" Yu-hsien answered by drawing his sword and slashing the bishop across the face.

Finally the Chinese Christians were brought forth to complete the carnage. Few escaped to report the tale of horror.

The bodies were left for the night where they had fallen and were stripped of clothing, rings and watches under cover of darkness. The next day the heads were placed in cages for a grotesque display on the city wall. Yu-hsien was without remorse and later crowed to the empress, "Your Majesty's slave caught them as in a net and allowed neither chicken nor dog to escape." The old woman replied, "You have done splendidly."

No Hiding Place

Eight British Baptist missionaries at Hsinchow, forty-five miles north of Taiyuan, heard the tragic news and decided to flee to the hills. They took refuge in caves where they were lovingly cared for by local Christians. Boxers roamed the area, seeking their hiding place. A Chinese evangelist was beaten to death for refusing to cooperate with the Boxers.

After their food supply was cut off, the missionaries received a message from the magistrate at Hsinchow offering them protection if they would return to the city. Upon arrival they were jailed about two weeks, then promised a protective armed escort to the coast. Rev. Herbert Dixon, one of the eight, told a Chinese preacher, "We are ready to glorify our Lord, by life or by death. If we die, there will certainly be others to take our place."

The Hsinchow eight set out in carts on August 8. As they were passing between the inner and outer gates of the city, their "escort" suddenly closed around them and other armed men sprang from hiding and brutally beat them all to death.

Massacre at Soping

At Soping ten missionaries of the small Swedish Holiness Union were holding their annual church conference in cooperation with Mr. and Mrs. Oscar Forsberg of the International Missionary Alliance Mission. Soping was already seething with unrest. Boxer agitators were saying that the missionaries had swept away approaching rain clouds with a yellow paper broom and that the foreigners were praying to their God that it might not rain.

According to Chinese evangelist Wang Lan-pu, who managed to escape, a mob converged on the house where the missionaries and Chinese Christians had barricaded themselves and began battering the door. Just as the mob burst into the house, the missionaries and their friends slipped out the back and ran to the city hall where they asked the magistrate for refuge. The Boxer leaders learned where they had gone and led the mob there. The magistrate refused to surrender his charges, but to pacify the howling crowd he said he had been ordered to send the foreigners to Peking where they would be executed. As the mob looked on, he had his blacksmith make manacles for five of the men. Apparently satisfied, the crowd dispersed.

Later than night the mob came back with soldiers sympathetic to the Boxers. Sparing no one, they stoned to death all the missionaries and their children along with Chinese Christians who had sought refuge. They hung the heads of the missionaries on the city wall as a ghastly testimonial to the populace. Among the Chinese who died were the mother and little daughter of the evangelist who escaped.

The June 29 massacre almost wiped out the tiny Swedish mission. Only two members in another province and one home on furlough were left. The senior Swedish martyr was Nathanael Carleson. Chinese believers had often used the scriptural allusion to introduce him: "Nathanael, an Israelite indeed, in whom is no guile." The youngest martyr was Ernst Petersson. He had been in China only five months. Four of the other eight were single women, all about thirty years of age. Aware of the danger of serving in bandit-ridden north China, Mina Hedlund, one of the four, had written in her last letter, "I don't fear if God wants me to suffer the death of a martyr."

Ambushed in the Desert

The International Missionary Alliance (now known as the Christian and Missionary Alliance—C&MA) had been founded by A.B. Simpson, a far-seeing Presbyterian minister with a vision for world evangelization. At the time of the Boxer uprising, this mission had about forty Swedish missionaries on the China field. At least nineteen adults and fifteen children met violent death.

The Olaf Bingmarks and their two young sons sensed trouble when children stopped coming to their school. Friends told them stories were spreading that Mr. Bingmark was extracting the eyes of Chinese boys for use as medicine. Duly warned, they kept inside their house. A peddler named Chao, whom they had kindly received many times, betrayed them for a price. Boxers dragged them outside and attacked them with swords and stones while an artist stood by sketching the violence. The picture, as later revealed, showed the two little boys kneeling and imploring mercy.

The Chinese evangelist who worked with them was bound for ten days without food and drink. Near death, his sufferings were mercifully ended by the sword.

Miss Gustafson, a beloved missionary teacher, lived alone at another station. When warned that Boxers were coming, she fled with another Chinese evangelist. A few miles down the road she was overtaken and stoned to death. Her body was thrown into a river and never seen again.

In far northwest China seven Alliance (C&MA) missionaries and seven children tried to flee on camels into Mongolia. Robbers intercepted them and took everything, even their clothes. In the trauma two of the missionaries gave birth. French missionary priests found the fourteen and the two infants naked in the desert and subsisting on roots. The priests gave them covering and took them back to the Catholic mission station.

News came that a Boxer army was approaching. "Our way ... is cut off," the Alliance's Carl Lundberg wrote. "If we are not able to escape, tell our friends we live and die for the Lord. I do not regret coming to China. The Lord has called me and His grace is sufficient. The way He chooses is

The Fury of the Boxers   19

best for me. His will be done. Excuse my writing, my hand is shivering."

Six days later he added, "The soldiers have arrived and will attack our place. The Catholics are prepared to defend themselves but it is in vain. We do not like to die with weapons in our hands. If it be the Lord's will let them take our lives."

When the Boxers attacked, the priests and two of the Alliance men, Emil Olson and Albert Anderson, tried to escape. They were captured, ordered to undress, then made to kneel for beheading. The others fared no better. The Boxers killed them with guns and swords, then set fire to the church.

Another seven Alliance missionaries with three children and four workers from other missions huddled in a chapel at Patzupupulong. Warned by the local magistrate that Boxers were on their way to kill them, the group set out for the coast. They ran into an ambush planned by the magistrate and all were killed except one of the wives. Left for dead, she was rescued and taken into the tent of a Mongol widow. However, the treacherous magistrate's wife learned where she was and sent soldiers to the tent. They murdered her in bed.

The Fatal Appointment

Most local Chinese officials were protective of missionaries. The magistrate at Fenchow in north Shansi was notably kind. Because of his friendliness, Mr. and Mrs. C.W. Price and other workers of the American Board of Commissioners of Foreign Missions invited three CIM colleagues, Mr. and Mrs. A.P. Lundren and Miss Annie Eldred, to come to stay with them during July when mob violence was at its peak. However, shortly after they arrived, the vindictive provincial governor appointed another magistrate to Fenchow. The new magistrate ordered the missionaries out of the city and assigned them an armed guard under the pretense of protection.

Apparently the missionaries expected the worst. Lizzie Atwater wrote her family on August 3:

> Dear ones, I long for a sight of your dear faces, but I
> fear we shall not meet on earth. . . . I am preparing
> for the end very quietly and calmly. The Lord is
> wonderfully near, and He will not fail me. I was very
> restless and excited while there seemed a chance of

life, but God has taken away that feeling, and now I just pray for grace to meet the terrible end bravely. The pain will soon be over, and oh the sweetness of the welcome above!

My little baby will go with me. I think God will give it to me in Heaven, and my dear mother will be so glad to see us. I cannot imagine the Savior's welcome. Oh, that will compensate for all these days of suspense. Dear ones, live near to God and cling less closely to earth. There is no other way by which we can receive that peace from God which passeth understanding. . . . I must keep calm and still these hours. I do not regret coming to China, but am sorry I have done so little. My married life, two precious years, has been so very full of happiness. We will die together, my dear husband and I.

I used to dread separation. If we escape now it will be a miracle. I send my love to you all, and the dear friends who remember me.

Twelve days later, when they were out of the area, the guards assigned by the new magistrate murdered the seven missionaries.

Detour to Death

Other trusting missionaries were betrayed by Boxer-inspired Chinese claiming to be their protectors. Such was the case of six CIM workers, two married couples and two single women, returning to their Shansi stations from vacations.

George McConnell, an Irish evangelist, and his Scottish wife Belle had buried their daughter in Scotland only two years before. They had just opened three new chapels and received fifty-one new inquirers. But the preacher sensed danger in the air. He quoted from Psalm 31 in a letter, " 'My times are in Thy hand.' "

John and Sarah Young had been married only fifteen months. He was Scottish, she an Indiana Hoosier. Both had made exceptional progress in the difficult Chinese language, but they lived one uncertain day at a time. In her application to CIM, Sarah had written, "I want to be found in the battle when He comes, and I want to be an instrument in the hands of God in saving souls from death." Eleven days before her martyrdom she wrote, "The winds may blow, and the waves may roll high; if we keep our eyes off them and on the Lord, we shall be all right. . . ."

Annie King and Elizabeth Burton, Britishers, were still single and strikingly attractive. They had been in China less than two years. Previous to her departure for China, Annie had been a home missionary, helping in the "Ragged Schools" for friendless child waifs in England. "Praise the Lord, I am really in China," she wrote home. "I don't know what the future holds for me, but, whatever comes, I know I have obeyed the will of our God." And later, "Often I wish I could have come before. . . . It is so nice to be in this village, where the people trust us, and love to hear of Jesus, for whose sake and the Gospel's we have come. There are numbers of villages where the name of Jesus is unknown, all in heathen darkness, without a ray of light."

Elizabeth, also a teacher, had written, "Oh, I feel so inadequate, so weak, and yet I hear Him say, 'Go in this thy might, have not I sent thee?' Yes, He has sent me; if ever I felt God has called me in my life, I feel it tonight." Then shortly before taking the fateful vacation: "Jesus is very real to me out in this land, and I would not change my present lot in spite of loneliness and occasional hardships."

Along the road to Yu-men-k'ou the group was met by soldiers who advised them to detour off the main road for safety. "We will accompany you," they said. Nearing the Yellow River, their escorts suddenly dismounted and unsheathed their swords. "You thought we came to protect you," the captain said. "Our orders are to kill you unless you promise to stop preaching your foreign religion." When the missionaries refused to so pledge, Mr. McConnell was pulled from his mule and decapitated with a quick swing of a sword. As Mrs. McConnell and their young son Kenneth hit the ground, the boy was heard to say, "Papa does not allow you to kill little Kennie." Swords flashed and two more heads rolled on the ground. The young women embraced each other as did the Youngs. Arms swung and death came quickly. The last to die was a faithful Chinese Christian servant, Kehtienhuen, who refused to deny his faith.

A Chinese Christian friend was able to escape. He smuggled a letter out describing the killings. "Men's hearts are shaking with fear," he reported. "We cannot rest day or night."

No Mercy Shown

At Ta-t'ung on June 24 CIM missionaries, two couples and their four children and two single women, took refuge with a friendly magistrate. The official defied the Boxer mob that circled the house clamoring for the blood of the foreigners. Then orders came on the twenty-seventh from a superior, ordering them to their home. The magistrate sent them under cover of darkness with an armed guard that remained at their door. A few days later Mrs. Stewart McKee gave birth. Now there were five children sheltered in the small house, while the mob outside grew noisier.

By July 12 only two guards remained. At seven o'clock that evening an official knocked and demanded the names of those inside. They were given.

An hour later three hundred soldiers arrived on horseback in support of the Boxers. Stewart McKee went out and tried to reason with them. Instead of listening, they hacked him to pieces, then set fire to the house. In the flames and confusion, only little Alice McKee managed to escape. In the morning the mob discovered her in a cowshed and slashed the defenseless child to death.

Buried in a Baptistry

The CIM's Emily Whitchurch and Edith Searell were one of many teams of young single women serving in isolated towns. Their only protection was the goodwill of the people.

They worked in Hsiao-i, a town in south central Shansi Province, with slaves of the terrible opium trade from which western nations were profiting. "Mornings and evenings," a visiting colleague wrote of Miss Whitchurch, "she would gather the opium patients around and teach them Scripture.... The Scriptures were as the voice of God to Miss Whitchurch; they shaped her life, and she had confidence in their power to purify and to convert."

Miss Searell was one of the first New Zealanders to come to China. In May she had been seriously ill with pleurisy, but refused to leave her British partner and Chinese friends. On June 28 she wrote a close friend, "From the human standpoint [all missionaries in Shansi Province] are equally unsafe. From the point of view of those whose lives are hid with Christ in God all are equally safe! His children shall have a place of refuge, and that place is the secret place of the Most High."

Two days later a Boxer mob attacked their house and showed them no mercy. After the mob left, loving Chinese Christians risked their lives in order to place the martyrs' bodies in a baptistry bordered with flowers which Miss Searell had planted a few weeks before.

No Earthly Sanctuary

No missionary was safe in Shansi Province. Scores were hidden by Chinese Christians at grave peril to their own lives.

"We will stand by you til death," Chinese friends vowed to the CIM's Duncan Kay, a colorful Scottish evangelist. "And we will stay until driven out," declared Kay.

When mobs threatened, Chinese believers spirited Kay, his wife and daughter Jenny, and three single women missionaries into the mountains and hid them in caves. With their help, Mrs. Kay was able to get a letter out to her three children at the CIM school in Chefoo, which was in a safe area in another province near the coast. She described their plight:

> [We are] being molested every day by bands of bad men who want money from us. Now our money is all gone. We feel there is nothing for us but to try and get back to the city; this is no easy matter. The roads are full of these bad people who seek our lives.
>
> I am writing this as it may be my last to you. Who knows but we may be with Jesus very soon. This is only a wee note to send our dear love to you all, and to ask you not to feel too sad when you know we have been killed. We have committed you all into God's hands. He will make a way for you all. Try and be good children. Love God. Give your hearts to Jesus. This is your dear parents' last request.
>
> Your loving papa, mama, and wee Jenny.

Shortly after the letter was sent, the three Kays were killed. The three young women, hiding in another cave, survived.

Another group of CIM missionaries were hidden in caves for three weeks before being captured by Boxers. "We are in God's hands," Willie Peat, who was accompanied by his wife Helen and two daughters and two single women, wrote. "I can say, 'I will fear no evil, for Thou art with me.'" One of the single women, nurse Edith Dobson, said in her last letter, "We know naught can come to us without His permission. So we have no need to be troubled: it is not in my nature to fear physical harm, but I trust, if it come, His grace will be all-sufficient."

They received a reprieve when a magistrate intervened and ordered a guard to deliver them to the town of K'u-wu. At K'u-wu a mob threatened, and they fled into nearby mountains. From their hideout in an earthen cave, Willie Peat wrote a last letter to his mother and uncle:

> The soldiers are just on us, and I have only time to say "Good-bye" to you all. We shall soon be with Christ, which is very far better for us. We can only now be sorry for you who are left behind and our dear native Christians.
> Goodbye! At longest it is only "til He come."
> We rejoice that we are made partakers of the sufferings of Christ, that when His glory shall be revealed we may "rejoice also with exceeding joy."

Helen Peat added, "Our Father is with us and we go to Him, and trust to see you all before His face, to be forever together with Him."

They were put to death on August 30.

Australian David Barratt, a veteran of only three years, was traveling when he heard of the Taiyuan massacre. "The news nearly made me faint," he wrote a colleague.

> The Empire is evidently upside down. No "Mene, mene, tekel, upharsin" is written on the old Middle Kingdom. Our blood may be as a true center (for the foundation) and God's kingdom will increase over this land. Extermination is but exaltation. God guide and bless us! "Fear not them which kill," He says, "are ye not of much more value than many sparrows." "Peace, perfect peace," to you, brother, and all at Lucheng. We may meet in the glory in a few hours or days.... Not a sleep, no dinner, a quiet time with God, then sunset and evening bells, then the dark.... Let us be true till death.

In such trusting faith the young Aussie was killed while seeking refuge on a desolate mountain.

Barratt's partner, Alfred Woodroofe, was at their station in Yo-yang when the persecution hit. The year before he had barely escaped a mob. Then he had written, "Are we called to die? The poor, feeble heart says, 'Oh, no; never.' But, to bring blessing into the world, what has it always meant?

What to the Savior? What to the Apostles? 'This is the way the Master went; should not the servant tread it still?'"

This time Woodroofe and three Chinese Christians were forced to flee into the mountains. For a week or more they slept in caves at night, retreating into remote canyons during the day. Woodroofe sent a message back to other believers in Yo-yang, stating his wish to return "so we can die together." The reply told him to remain hidden. He wrote again, describing how his feet were cut and bleeding from wandering among the rocks, but ended by quoting James 5:11: "We count them happy that endure." This was his last message. He died at age twenty-eight.

Details of how he and about a dozen other CIM workers died were not known for many months. The few who managed to slip letters out expressed similar courage and faith and wished only that the Chinese church would be strengthened through their martyrdom. Wrote Edith Nathan, who served with her sister May and with Mary Heaysman at Ta-ning: "I hope I shan't be ordered off anywhere; if my Christians are in trouble, I trust I may be allowed to stay and help. One does long for the native Church to be on the right foundation—Christ Jesus." Mary Heaysman headed her last letter, "There shall be showers of blessing." The three young women and ten Chinese believers were captured after a long and harrowing flight and put to death in a pagan temple.

Journeys of Death

In the most terrible of the flights, two parties of missionaries fled from Shansi Province to the city of Hankow in Hupeh Province a thousand miles south.

One group of fourteen included two families with six young children and four single women fleeing from the town of Lucheng. Mobs followed them from one village boundary to the next, hurling sticks and stones, shouting, "Death to the foreign devils!" Robbers stripped them of everything but a few rags. Emaciated from hunger and thirst, shoeless, barebacked in the scorching heat, desperately trying to hold up filthy, torn Chinese trousers, they staggered from village to village half alive.

The young children displayed remarkable insight and faith. "If they loved Jesus they would not do this," seven-year-old Jessie Saunders reminded her parents. Once when they took shelter in a barn, the now fever-stricken child looked up at her mother who was fanning her and said, "Jesus was born in a place like this."

A few days later Jessie's baby sister, Isabel, died from beatings and exposure to the hot sun. As Jessie grew weaker, she cried for a place of rest. Her wish was granted a week after Isabel's death. The two children were buried beside the road.

In one village attackers dragged one of the men, E.J. Cooper, into the open country and left him for dead. He somehow revived and crawled back to his family and friends. Margaret (Mrs. E.J.) Cooper began lapsing into unconsciousness. Once she whispered to her husband, an architect whom she had married after joining the CIM, "If the Lord spares us, I should like to go back to Lucheng if possible." But her beatings were too severe, and she slipped into merciful death.

On July 12 Hattie Rice collapsed in the heat. A mob began stoning her and a man ran a cart over her naked body to break her spine. Her companion, Mary Huston, shielded her body until shamefaced men came with clothing. When she was again clothed, they took her from Miss Huston to a temple and consulted their gods about her faith. When a priest announced that the gods would let her live, the men carried her back to the other missionaries on a stretcher. She died a short time later.

The survivors somehow kept moving. They crossed and recrossed the Yellow River. They were imprisoned and released. Miss Huston suffered the worst. Part of her brain was exposed from beatings received at the time Miss Rice had been fatally wounded. Her friends could do no more for her than protect her from the sun. She died on August 11. Both young women were from the United States, Miss Rice from Massachusetts and Miss Huston from Pennsylvania. Assigned to a refuge for opium addicts, they had taken nothing from China and given everything.

Shortly before Miss Huston's death, the Lucheng group had met and joined a second group. Led by the CIM's Archibald Glover, they told a harrowing story of beatings, imprisonments and miraculous deliverance. Mrs. Glover was in her last month of pregnancy. The last leg of their journey was made together by boat, allowing them to take the bodies of Mrs. Cooper and Miss Huston to Hankow for burial.

Three days after their arrival, Mr. Cooper laid his tiny son Brainerd beside his wife. He then wrote his own mother:

> The Lord has honored us by giving us fellowship in His sufferings. Three times stoned, robbed of everything, even clothes, we know what hunger, thirst, nakedness, weariness are as never before, but also the sustaining grace and strength of God and His peace in a new and deeper sense than before. . . .
>
> Billow after billow has gone over me. Home gone, not one memento of dear Maggie even, penniless, wife and child gone to glory, Edith [his other child] lying very sick with diarrhea and your son weak and exhausted to a degree, though otherwise well. . . .
>
> And now that you know the worst, Mother, I want to tell you that the cross of Christ, that exceeding glory of the Father's love, has brought continual comfort to my heart, so that not one murmur has broken the peace of God within.

The Peril at Paoting

Outside of Shansi Province the worst Boxer massacre of missionaries occurred at Paoting, then capital of the adjoining province Chihli (now Hopeh Province), where American (Northern) Presbyterians, the CIM, and the American Board of Commissioners for Foreign Missions had stations.

On June 1 CIM workers H.V. Robinson and C. Norman were seized and killed by Boxers outside the old walled city. The gates were heavily guarded, sealing off any possible escape by the eight remaining missionaries, four children, and the Chinese believers inside Paoting.

A story was circulated that the missionaries had poisoned the dwindling water supply in the wells. Another rumor charged that the Presbyterian's Dr. G.B. Taylor was extracting the eyes of children for medicine. Still another lie said the missionaries had helped build the hated railway that had taken jobs from cargo haulers.

The last letter out stated, "Our position is dangerous—very. We are having awfully hot, dry dusty days and *yao yen* [rumors] are increasing. . . . Oh that God would send rain. That would make things quiet for a time. . . . We can't go out and fight—we must sit still, do our work, and if God calls us to Him, that's all. Unless definite orders come from

28   MARTYRS OF CHINA

Peking that we are to be protected at any cost or a guard of foreign soldiers sent at once, the blood must flow. We are trying to encourage the [Chinese] brethren, but it is difficult work. A crisis must come soon—the Lord's will be done."

In this situation two friends managed to enter the city. One was Pastor Meng, the first Chinese to be ordained by the American Board's North China Mission. The missionaries begged him to leave. As a Chinese he could melt into the constant flow of human traffic and go to a safer town. "No," he vowed, "I will keep the church open as long as God allows. And after I am with the Lord, my son will keep it open."

The second arrival, Rev. William Cooper, deputy director of the CIM, had been visiting mission stations in adjoining Shansi Province and was returning to the metropolis of Tientsin on the coast. Like a Paul Revere, he had been warning missionaries at stations along the way, enabling some to escape just in time. Now he was caught.

Cooper was an old China hand, having been on the field nineteen years. A long bout with typhoid had impaired his hearing, but his spiritual senses remained strong. "One of the very few blameless lives I have ever come into contact with," declared a missionary friend. "He lived in an atmosphere of prayer," said another. "He literally drew breath in the fear of the Lord." In Paoting he joined CIM colleagues Benjamin and Emily Bagnall and their five-year-old daughter Gladys.

At the American Board station were H.T. Pitkin, Miss A.A. Gould, and Miss M.S. Morrill. Pitkin was one of the great missionary spirits of China. A classmate of Henry Luce (who later founded *Time* magazine) and Sherwood Eddy, Pitkin had served as secretary of the vigorous Student Missionary Movement before manning the American Board's mission station at Paoting.

On Saturday, June 30, the American Presbyterian Mission in the northern part of the city was attacked. Dr. Taylor went outside to plead that the missionaries had come to China only to do good. He was killed almost immediately and his head displayed in a pagan temple. After disposing of Dr. Taylor, the Boxer-led soldiers set the Presbyterian mission house on fire. One of the men, Frank Simcox, was seen walking to and fro on the veranda, holding the hands of his two sons as the flames enveloped them.

News of the martyrdom of the Presbyterians traveled rapidly to the other mission houses on the south side. The three members of the American Board, Pastor Meng, and other Chinese Christians kept a vigil through the night, writing last letters to loved ones, letters which would later be dug up by Boxers and destroyed. When morning dawned the Chinese, at the urging of the missionaries, slipped out the back door. About nine o'clock the Boxers arrived.

Miss Morrill went out to plead with the soldiers. "Kill me and let the others go," she begged. "I am ready to die for them." Her entreaty, according to the later report of one of the soldiers, touched off an argument in the crowd. Some of the older Boxers and the soldiers wanted to spare the four. The others wanted to proceed with the killing. During the controversy the missionaries were allowed to remain in their house.

The hard-liners won the dispute. Pitkin was killed defending the women. Miss Gould died of shock before the attackers could reach her. Miss Morrill was captured alive and taken to a pagan temple where William Cooper and the Bagnall family had already been taken.

Throughout Sunday they were taunted and abused as objects of sport and mockery. That evening they were taken out for execution. Mrs. Bagnall begged in vain for the life of her daughter while the cherubic-faced child with long golden curls stood by in frightened perplexity. The plea was refused, and at the captain's command they were all beheaded.

Murders in Mongolia

The dark hand of Boxer hate reached even into bleak Mongolia. Once the fountainhead of the great Mongol Empire, the high, thinly populated desert nation was in 1900 a vassal state of China. Christian work was so difficult that mission boards hesitated to send their missionaries there, and it came to be called "the neglected field."

In 1895 the Scandinavian Alliance Mission of Chicago (now The Evangelical Alliance Mission—TEAM) sent its first worker, a red-bearded Swede. Taking a cue from pioneer James Gilmour, "the apostle to Mongolia," David Stenberg clad himself in woolen Mongolian skirts, rode a camel, traveled with the nomadic shepherd people, ate their food and learned their language. Within three years he received support from five other hardy Scandinavian missionaries—N.J.

Friedstrom, Carl Suber, Hanna Lund, and Hilda and Clara Anderson. Upon finding Stenberg, they mistook him for a Mongolian.

In the spring of 1900 they heard the rumors of danger to foreigners in China. Such rumors were common and they were from far off. They gave them little consideration.

In September they embarked on a long journey. A half-day out they met a Mongol who advised them to turn back. Stenberg and the women went on under the protection of a Mongol chief. Friedstrom and Suber waited awhile, then fearing danger decided Friedstrom should search for their friends while Suber remained with the caravan. When Friedstrom did not return, Suber became alarmed and sent a friendly Mongol to investigate. He came back in two weeks with horrifying news. The chief had betrayed them. Following orders from Peking, he had sent them to a lonely spot in the desert where soldiers killed them, then preserved their heads in salt for shipment to Peking where an award was expected. Weeks later, another Mongol led Suber to the spot where the only visible remains were a blonde curl and a shoe among ashes.

The Merciless Vegetarians

The extent of the Boxer persecutions in north China and Mongolia obscured bloodshed elsewhere by other rebellious groups. The worst violence occurred at Ku-chau in south central Chekiang Province where the Kiang-san, a secret vegetarian society similar to the Boxers, had launched an anti-foreign, anti-Christian vendetta. It was in this province that CIM founder Hudson Taylor had commenced work in 1857.

Three hundred federal soldiers had been sent to calm the agitated populace and to protect CIM missionaries D. Baird and Agnes Thompson and their two young sons, Edith Sherwood, Etta Manchester, and Josephine Desmond. The protectors were a joke. They had come without arms.

"We hear all kinds of evil reports which make us fear," Thompson wrote, "but by His grace we are able to rise above all, and take hold of our God and Savior.... We will just 'stand still and see the salvation of God.' ... His will be done."

The five workers were among the best the CIM had in China. The Thompsons had not taken a furlough in fifteen years. In the Ku-chau area they had established a bustling church with a strong evangelistic outreach. Almost every night, Scotsman Thompson and national evangelists held services. Mrs. Thompson was instructing eighty Chinese women twice weekly.

Nurse Josephine Desmond, an Irish American from Massachusetts, had trained at Moody's Bible Training School in Chicago under R.A. Torrey. Miss Desmond had been caring for her co-worker Etta Manchester, a New Yorker who had been in China only three years. Friends had implored her to return home. She replied: "I am willing to come home if that is what God wants. If He wants me to remain here, I will stay. I am prepared to do the will of God, whatever the cost."

At forty-six Edith Sherwood was the eldest of the single women. She had been influenced by the Thompsons to leave missionary work in Europe and come to China. A friend had called her "a center of hope and love to old and young."

Reports from Chinese Christians described the missionaries' martyrdom. A mob attacked the mission house on July 21, wounding Thompson. Edith Sherwood and Etta Manchester ran to seek help from the magistrate and arrived as he was being led to execution. Chinese friends pulled them aside just in time and directed them to a secret hiding place.

The mob succeeded in breaking down the missionaries' door that afternoon. Helpless to resist, the Thompsons, their two children, and Miss Desmond were put to death immediately. Three days later Miss Sherwood and Miss Manchester were discovered and killed.

Around the same time three other CIM missionaries were about twenty miles away, trying to reach a hoped-for haven in Ku-chau. Britisher George Ward and his wife Etta, an Iowan, had met and married on the field. The number of Chinese believers at their station in Ch'ang-shan had doubled in three years. Their companion, Emma Thirgood, was still weak from a long illness that had kept her in England for three years. She had amazed everyone by returning to China the year before.

Upon learning that the Kiang-san were in close pursuit, they decided to split into parties. Mrs. Ward and Miss Thirgood boarded a boat with the hope that they would be safer as unprotected women. They were killed at a river jetty. Mr. Ward was caught and murdered about five miles from Ku-chau.

The Fellowship of Blood

More evangelical Protestant missionaries were killed in the Boxer bloodbath than Catholic representatives from abroad. The Catholics were often able to barricade themselves in fortress-like cathedrals. Chinese casualties, however, were just the reverse. Thirty thousand Catholics perished, while only two thousand Protestants gave their lives. Many thousands more lost all their property to burning, looting mobs who systematically sought out residences of persons listed on church registers.

Stories of bravery abound.

At P'ing-tu, Shantung Province, some twenty native Christians were seized and offered escape if they would deny their God and worship the idols. When they refused, their queues were tied to the tails of horses, and they were dragged twenty-five miles to Lai-chou where most were killed.

At Ta-t'ung, in Shansi Province, where six missionaries and five children died, eighteen Chinese believers offered themselves for baptism while the Boxer storm was mounting. Five died with the missionaries a few days afterward.

At another town in Shansi, one man who at first had denied Christ later repented and told the Boxer magistrate, "I cannot but believe in Christ: even if you put me to death, I will still believe and follow Him." For this he was beaten to death, his body cut open, and his heart extracted and exhibited in the magistrate's office.

At the town of Honchau, also in bloody Shansi, "Faithful" Yen and his wife were tied to a pillar in the pagan temple. After beating them with rods, the Boxers lit a fire behind them and burned their legs raw. Although they still would not deny Christ, Mrs. Yen was set free. But Mr. Yen was thrown to the ground and firewood stacked around him. The fire was lit. After a few minutes of roasting in agony, he tried to roll out of the fire. A Boxer began to heap his body with hot ashes and coals. A soldier standing by could stand it no longer and cursed the Boxer. The Boxers leaped on the soldier and cut him to pieces. At that, the other soldiers rushed on the Boxers and chased them out of the temple. They then took the pitifully burned Chinese Christian from the fire and carried him still alive to the magistrate's house, only to see the official throw the man in a dark prison cell where it is presumed he died.

At Taiyuan, after the foreigners were beheaded, many of the Chinese Christians were forced to kneel down and drink their blood. Some also had crosses burned into their foreheads.

Here, a mother and her two children were kneeling before the executioner when a watcher suddenly ran and pulled the children back into the anonymity of the observing crowd. Taken by surprise, the Boxers were unable to find either the man or the children. They then turned back to the mother and asked if she had any last word. Dazed, she begged to see the face of the kind man who had taken her children. The man came forward in tears at risk of his life. Satisfied that the children would be cared for, the mother went to her death because she would not deny her Lord.

In the Hsinchow district, where eight English Baptist missionaries were killed, a Christian family—Chao Hsi Mao, his wife, sister, and mother—were driven to their place of execution in a large open cart. As they were pushed along they sang the hymn, "He Leadeth Me." When everything was ready, each in turn was asked to recant. One by one they bravely refused and were beheaded.

At Fang-ssu, another British Baptist station, the small church building was burned by the Boxers and the young minister Chou Yung-yao beaten nearly to death for refusing to divulge the names and whereabouts of his flock. As the mob began dragging him toward the flames, he shouted, "You need not drag me. I will go myself." He crawled into the blazing ruins. A moment later the roof collapsed over him to crown his final act of devotion to Christ.

About one hundred Chinese Christians were rounded up in the Shou-yang district, among them fourteen members of one family, and given a test of faith. A large circle was drawn on the ground and a cross inscribed in the center. To indicate their denial of Christ, all they had to do was step outside the circle. Only a few accepted this invitation. Those that stood their ground included a sizable number of teenagers. All were killed.

In a village in Shansi, another mother, Mrs. Meng, was weaving cloth on her household loom when a crowd of fierce faces appeared in her doorway. She knew who they were and what they wanted even before the inevitable question, "Will you deny your belief in Jesus?" "Wait a moment, please," she calmly replied. She stepped down from her loom and went to the closet where her family's best clothing was kept for holidays and funerals and donned her best gown. Then she walked to the door and knelt. "Now you may do as you wish, for I will not deny Jesus." A command, a flash of steel in the air, and the deed was done.

In the mountains nine Black Miao tribal Christian men, the first believers of their tribe, were called before the headman of their village on a ruse. One of the nine, sensing a trap, slipped away. Seven of the eight who appeared were seized and beheaded without trial or defense. In the days following, twenty-seven other Miao Christians were martyred and hundreds fined and forbidden to speak to one another.

In a church in Honan Province the Boxers took the rollbook and went around to one hundred homes, offering each family immunity from persecution if they would renounce their faith and worship idols. Ninety-nine stood fast. Their homes were looted, their cornfields trampled down, their farm implements stolen, their cattle driven off, and they were left destitute.

A young teacher near the Great Wall was left in charge of seventeen schoolgirls in a boarding school when the missionary had to leave. Influential people offered to hide her, but she refused to leave the girls who could not get to their homes. Hiding in fields and caves, they were hunted like wild animals. Finally they were captured and led to a Boxer temple for execution.

A Christian cook was seized and beaten, his ears were cut off, his mouth and cheeks slashed with a sword, and other shameful mutilations afflicted. He remained true.

A Chinese preacher who refused to apostatize was given a hundred blows on his bare back and then asked again to deny Christ. "No, never," the half-dead man of God declared. "I value Jesus Christ more than life and I will never deny Him!" Before the second hundred blows were completed, he collapsed and his tormentors left thinking he was dead. A friend stealthily carried him away, bathed his wounds, and secretly nursed him to recovery.

No Chinese Christian was safe from the Boxer wrath, not even the most highly educated. Dr. Wang was one of the first graduates from the Peking University Medical School.

When he and his little son were arrested, Boxers told him, "Dr. Wang, you are an educated man. We do not want to kill you, but we have no choice unless you burn incense to the gods."

"No, I cannot do that," he replied.

"We'll make it easy for you," the Boxers offered. "Get someone to burn incense in your place."

When he again refused, they offered to find him a substitute. "You will only have to go to the temple with us," they said.

"No, I will not," he persisted. "You may kill me, but I will not worship your gods in any way. There are four generations of Christians in my family. Do you think I would let this child see his father deny his Savior? Kill me if you must, but I will not betray my Lord."

They ran him through with a sword, lamenting, "What a pity to kill such a man."

The bravery of such Christians astounded the Boxers. Sometimes they ripped out the hearts of victims in search of the secret of their courage. Finding nothing but flesh, they would then remark, "It was the medicine of the foreign devils [the missionaries]."

The Bravery of Blind Chang

Of all the Chinese martyrs none died with more courage than Blind Chang, the most famous evangelist in Manchuria, homeland of the Manchu rulers of China.

Chang Shen had been converted after being stricken blind in mid-life. Before his conversion he had been known as *Wu so pu wei te,* meaning, "one without a particle of good in him." A gambler, woman-chaser and thief, he had driven his wife and only daughter from home. When he was stricken blind, neighbors said it was the judgment of the gods for his evil doing.

Chang heard of a missionary hospital where people were receiving sight. In 1886 he traveled overland for hundreds of miles to reach the hospital, only to be told every bed was full. The hospital evangelist took pity and gave up his own bed. Chang's eyesight was partially restored, and he heard about Christ for the first time. "Never had we a patient who received the gospel with such joy," reported the doctor.

When Chang asked for baptism, missionary James Webster replied, "Go home and tell your neighbors that you have changed. I will visit you later and if you are still following Jesus, then I will baptize you."

Five months later Webster arrived in Chang's area and found hundreds of inquirers. He baptized the new evangelist with great joy.

A clumsy native doctor robbed Chang of the little eyesight the missionaries had restored. No matter—Chang continued his travels from village to village, winning hundreds more, praising God when cursed and spit upon, even when ferocious dogs were turned loose to drive him away. He learned practically the whole New Testament by memory and could quote entire chapters from the Old Testament. Missionaries followed after him, baptizing converts and organizing churches.

When the Boxer fury arose, Chang was preaching at Tsengkow, Manchuria. Christians felt sure he would be one of the first targets and led him to a cave in the mountains.

The Boxers reached the nearby city called Ch'ao-yang-shan first and rounded up about fifty Christians for execution. "You're fools to kill all these," a resident told them. "For every one you kill, ten will spring up while that man Chang Shen lives. Kill him and you will crush the foreign religion." The Boxers promised to spare the fifty if someone would take them to Chang. No one volunteered. Finally when it appeared the Boxers would kill the fifty, one man slipped away and found Chang to tell him what was happening. "I'll gladly die for them," Chang offered. "Take me there."

When Chang arrived, the Boxer leaders were at another town. Nevertheless, he was bound by local authorities and taken to the temple of the god of war, and commanded to worship.

"I can only worship the One Living and True God," he declared.

"Then repent," they cried.

"I repented many years ago."

"Then believe in Buddha."

"I already believe in the one true Buddha, even Jesus Christ."

"You must at least bow to the gods."

"No. Turn my face toward the sun." Chang knew that at this time of day the sun was shining toward the temple and his back would be to the idols. When they turned him around, he knelt and worshiped the God of the Bible.

Three days later the Boxer leaders arrived. The blind evangelist was put in an open cart and driven to the cemetery outside the city wall. As he passed through the crowds, he sang the first Christian song he had learned at the hospital.

> Jesus loves me, He who died
> Heaven's gate to open wide;
> He will wash away my sin,
> Let His little child come in.
>
> Jesus loves me, He will stay,
> Close beside me all the way;
> If I love Him when I die,
> He will take me home on high.

When they reached the cemetery, he was shoved into a kneeling position. Three times he cried, "Heavenly Father, receive my spirit." Then the sword flashed, and his head tumbled to the ground.

The Boxers refused to let the Christians bury his body. Instead, fearful of a report that Blind Chang would rise from the dead, they forced the believers to buy oil and burn the mangled remains. Even so, the Boxers became afraid and fled from the revenge which they believed Chang's spirit would wreak upon them. The local Christians were thus spared persecution.

The Tribulation in Peking

The largest number of Chinese Christians died in the populous cities of Peking and Tientsin. Fewer died in Tientsin where a young Quaker engineer named Herbert Hoover, the future president of the United States, and other foreigners gave them refuge and the opportunity to help defend the foreign garrison against attacks by Chinese government soldiers.

But not a single missionary died in Tientsin. And only one was martyred in Peking, an Englishman known as Professor James who had been in the country since 1883. As the crisis was developing, he went out to check on Chinese Christian friends. Soldiers captured him and took him to the house of two of the leaders in the coup that had overthrown Emperor Kuang-hsu. They ordered him to kneel. The missionary refused, declaring, "I cannot kneel to anyone but my

God and King." Then he was forced to kneel upon a chain for several hours. He was executed three days later and his head exhibited in a cage hanging from the beam of the Tung An Gate.

The foreigners in Peking were fast gathering in the British ambassador's compound for protection against sniper attacks. Unexpectedly, the empress' troop commander in the capital announced a short truce to permit all the foreigners to take shelter. American Methodist missionaries begged their ambassador to wait for seven hundred Chinese Christian girls who were unprotected in their mission school a mile away. "We appeal to you in the name of humanity and Christianity not to abandon them," the missionary said. The ambassador felt the risk was too great. Missionary Frank Gamewell then warned that "our Christian nation will never live down your decision." Gamewell and his colleagues could only go back and distribute money to students and faculty and instruct them to hide wherever they could.

After the foreigners were safely behind the walls of the British compound, the Boxers and their fanatical supporters struck. The tragedy they inflicted was described by Dr. George Ernest Morrison of the London *Times* who was caught in Peking:

> As darkness came on the most awful cries were heard in the city, most demoniacal and unforgettable, the cries of the Boxers—*Sha kuei-tzu* [kill the devils]—mingled with the shrieks of the victims and the groans of the dying. For Boxers were sweeping through the city, massacring the native Christians and burning them alive in their homes. The first building to be burned was the chapel of the Methodist Mission in the Hatamen Street. Then flames sprang up in many quarters of the city. Amid the most deafening uproar, the Tung-tang or East Cathedral shot flames into the sky. The old Greek Church in the northeast of the city, the London Mission buildings, the handsome pile of the American Board Mission, and the entire foreign buildings belonging to the Imperial Marine Customs in the east city burned throughout the night. It was an appalling sight.
>
> ... On June 15th rescue parties were sent out by the American and Russian Legations in the morning, and by the British and German Legations in the after-

noon, to save if possible native Christians from the burning ruins.... Awful sights were witnessed. Women and children hacked to pieces, men trussed like fowls, with noses and ears cut off and eyes gouged out. Chinese Christians accompanied the reliefs and ran about in the labyrinth of network of streets that formed the quarter, calling upon the Christians to come out from their hiding places. All through the night the massacre had continued, and Boxers were even now shot red-handed at their bloody work. As the patrol was passing a Taoist Temple on the way, a noted Boxer meeting place, cries were heard within. The temple was forcibly entered. Native Christians were found there, their hands tied behind their backs, awaiting execution and torture, some had already been put to death, and their bodies were still warm and bleeding. All were shockingly mutilated. Their fiendish murderers were at their incantations burning incense before their gods, offering Christians in sacrifice to their angered deities.

Several hundred Chinese Christians did reach the besieged foreigners and worked heroically digging ditches and fortifying the walls against Boxer attacks. As the first shells burst over the walls, Chinese children could be heard singing, "There'll be no dark valley when Jesus comes." Finally in August an international rescue force, marching from Tientsin, reached Peking and broke the siege. By this time the Chinese Christians were reduced to eating leaves. Arm and leg bones protruded through their skin, and they were too weak to cheer their rescuers.

The empress was overthrown and fled Peking in terror. Many of her advisers committed suicide. The victorious foreign expeditionary force allowed a caretaker government to take over. Now the Boxers became the hunted, and thousands were killed by foreign and Chinese troops. The mad governor of Shansi Province was beheaded.

The Last Boxer Martyr

Meanwhile, the CIM missionaries who had been beaten on long marches were being cared for in hospitals. Mrs. Glover gave birth to the child she had carried on her thousand mile trek. But tiny Faith Edith lived only ten days.

Mrs. Glover helped plan the burial service, choosing one of the CIM's favorite hymns which begins, "Hark, hark the song the ransomed sing." After the burial, Mrs. Glover's health improved and she was moved to Shanghai. There she took a sharp turn for the worse and began sinking fast. Late on the afternoon of October 24, she picked up the lines of "Jesus, Lover of My Soul" which her husband had been singing by her bedside. In a remarkably clear voice she sang,

    Leave, ah! leave me not alone,
    Still support and comfort me.

At four the next morning she was with Christ.

She was the last of the Shansi missionary martyrs to die. As her coffin was lowered, her husband, two sons who had been away at school, and missionary and Chinese friends sang the hymn she had sung so many times to her children at bedtime:

    Sun of my soul, Thou Savior dear,
    It is not night if Thou be near.

Afterwards her husband had inscribed on her headstone two praise notes appropriate to all the martyrs of the Boxer uprising:

THE NOBLE ARMY OF MARTYRS PRAISE THEE.
IN THY PRESENCE IS FULNESS OF JOY.

The Power and the Glory

The Boxers had inflicted the most severe blow ever dealt to the modern Protestant missionary movement launched by William Carey. A total of 135 missionaries and 53 children had been killed—100 from Britain and Commonwealth nations, 56 from Sweden, and 32 from the United States. Of this number, 79 were associated with the CIM and 36 with the C&MA, the societies which suffered the greatest losses. Many China watchers thought Protestants were finished in China. Chinese believers, they said, are rice Christians and the native church will fade away. They further predicted that missionaries would never again be welcome in China.

The doomsayers were wrong on all counts.

When the rebellion was over, an assessment showed that the Chinese church had been battered but had never bent. For example, the Methodists in Foochow met after the missionaries had departed and agreed they would continue their educational and evangelistic work, even if they never received another missionary or dollar of mission money.

When peace and order came and the missionaries returned, a delegation of twelve men came from a village to ask for a Christian preacher. "We want to know more about your religion. We will support the minister and provide him a place to live and a building in which to preach."

At Taiyuan the remains of the slain missionaries and Chinese Christians were carefully gathered up and buried in the Martyr Memorial Cemetery. Later a Martyr Memorial Church was opened at the spot where Miss Coombs had been burned to death while trying to rescue two of her Chinese students. A memorial stone, on which was inscribed the names of the Taiyuan martyrs, was placed on the porch of the new church.

At Paoting, where two hospitals were built as memorials to the slain missionary doctors, the commander of the Chinese Second Army Division, General Wang, came to the Presbyterian mission and requested Christian teachers to come to instruct his men in the gospel and biblical morality.

Powerful, soul-cleansing revivals surged across north China. Missionaries confessed sins of arrogance, pride and ill feeling toward their co-workers and asked forgiveness. Chinese pastors and church leaders confessed failures to their flocks. Kinsmen who had been long estranged made tearful reconciliations. Prodigals came and knelt at their parents' feet and begged forgiveness. Many parents asked their children for forgiveness. The Methodist's Bishop Cassels recorded:

Scoffers might call the work by an evil name; unbelievers might laugh at the unusual scenes; hard hearts might for a time resist the influence; but those whose eyes were opened and whose hearts were touched, felt indeed that now, if never before, they had been brought into touch with the powers of the other world, and with the mighty working of the Spirit of God.

Protestants more than doubled during the six years following the massacres. In 1901 one missionary in Kiangsi Province reported twenty thousand converts.

Throughout China there was mass interest in Christianity. It was well-known that most Christians, Chinese and foreign, had not demanded indemnities for loss of life and destruction of property as other foreigners had. Hudson Taylor, director of the missionary society which had suffered most, asked CIM workers to show to the Chinese "the meekness and gentleness of Christ, not only not to enter any claim against the Chinese Government but to refrain from accepting compensation even if offered." In Shansi Province, where the greatest damage had been wreaked, newly appointed officials appointed Baptist missionary Timothy Richard to help make post-Boxer adjustments. Richard suggested that a large sum be set aside as an indemnity, not to be paid foreigners but to found in Taiyuan a Chinese university. He believed this would help dispel the ignorance and superstition which had enabled the Boxers to gain support from the populace. The proposal was accepted and another English Baptist missionary was appointed the first principal.

Chinese church leaders more than matched the spirit of the missionaries. Even those who had lost loved ones exhibited remarkable restraint and foregiveness. Chen Wei-ping, pastor of the Asbury Methodist Church in Peking, had lost his minister father and mother and sister to crazed Boxers in Yen-ching-chou. His father had been beheaded, his mother and thirteen-year-old sister hacked to pieces as they clung in each other's arms. When invited by the government to submit a claim, Pastor Chen replied, "We are not in need. We do not want payment." Instead he requested his bishop to "Appoint me to Yen-ching-chou that I may preach the message of love to the men who killed my loved ones." The bishop consented.

The families of the missionary martyrs were equally forgiving. Sherwood Eddy, the missionary statesman, told a student missionary convention in Kansas City about visiting the parents of Mrs. E.R. Atwater in Oberlin, Ohio. She, her husband, and their four children had been killed by soldiers who had pretended to be their protectors. Recalled Eddy, "They said, in tears, 'We do not begrudge them—we gave them to that needy land; China will yet believe the truth.'"

Sending churches were challenged by missionary and Chinese speakers fresh from China to embark on a crash program for evangelizing China. Yale student Fei Chi-hao told another student missionary convention, "My parents are now wearing the martyr's crown in the 'Home above.' It is my ambition to follow in the footsteps of your missionaries and carry back the blessed message to my people." Then he challenged the students about China's immediate needs. "We need colleges and universities, railroads and factories,"

The Fury of the Boxers 43

he said. "But the thing that we need most, just now, is Christianity. The Christian religion is the only hope and salvation of China."

Such appeals brought wave after wave of new missionaries to China and millions of dollars for evangelization and education.

The Boxer martyrdoms in China bore fruit for decades following. Thousands upon thousands came to Christ as a direct result of the slaughter of Christians in 1900. Some had been direct observers of persecutions and could not, as Saul of Tarsus in witnessing the stoning of Stephen, forget the bravery and dedication of those who had died.

One of the most notable was Feng Yu-hsiang, the soldier who watched the murders at Paoting. In 1913, as a major, he professed faith in Christ at an evangelistic meeting led by John R. Mott in Peking. Afterwards he testified, "I saw Miss Morrill offer her life for her friends. And a missionary walking with his sons on a veranda in calmness and peace while flames rose to envelop them. I could never forget that."

Feng Yu-hsiang became China's most famous "Christian General." He won hundreds of his officers to Christ, forbade gambling and prostitution in his camps, and had his men taught useful trades.

The results were much less spectacular in Mongolia where the Scandinavian missionaries had given their all. But their successors were confident. Said Mrs. A.B. Magnuson:

> Looking back on our work in Mongolia it seems
> dark, having borne little fruit, but I lift my eyes
> upward to Him who can look deeper and farther than
> we can look and does not judge simply by the outward appearance as we do. He can change and transform all things and no work for Him is in vain. We
> believe there will be some saved souls from Mongolia in the great blood-washed multitude before the
> throne of the Redeemer. "They that sow in tears
> shall reap in joy."

The defeat of the Boxers and their Imperial backer marked a turning point in China's history. The feudal Manchu dynasty was soon overthrown and the Chinese Republic founded under the leadership of Sun Yat-sen, a Christian whose life had once been saved by a British missionary.

The new generation of Chinese looked to the "Christian" West for education and technical aid. Protestant missionaries were invited to start universities in every major city. By 1911 most Chinese political leaders were Protestants, including Sun Yat-sen. One official even suggested that Christianity be made the state religion.

NO ARK OF SAFETY:
China in the Following Decades

The Boxer defeat opened China to greater evangelization, but it did not mark the end of violence. Scores of missionaries and thousands of Chinese Christians were martyred in the line of duty during the next half century. Most were killed by mobs, dread diseases, Japanese bombs and bullets, and Communist assassination squads — all before the Red scourge enveloped the Celestial Kingdom and cut off communication with Christianity abroad.

Superstition and ignorance continued to spur the dark horse of death. In the summer of 1902 a cholera epidemic swept parts of north China. Thirteen children died at the CIM's Chefoo school where missionaries sent their school-age youngsters. One was the son of Boxer martyrs, Mr. and Mrs. Duncan Kay. Missionaries at their stations were working to save thousands of Chinese when a rumor was circulated that they were spreading the epidemic with their poison (medicine). In Chen-chou, Honan Province, two CIM members, J.R. Bruce of Australia and R.H. Lowis of England, were attacked by a fear-ridden mob and murdered as a result of the rumor.

The Doctor's Devotion

Anti-foreign mobs continued to lengthen the trail of blood of the Christian missionaries, who were not ordinary foreigners but humanitarians of the highest order. Dr. Eleanor Chestnut, an orphan girl from Waterloo, Iowa, is an example. An orphan raised by a poor aunt in the backwoods of Missouri, she skimped and starved to get through Park College, dressing in castoffs from the missionary barrel. Determined to be a medical missionary, she lived in an attic and ate mostly oatmeal while attending medical school in Chicago. To earn money she nursed the aged. She was nurse to Dr. Oliver Wendell Holmes in his final illness.

After studies at Moody Bible Institute, Dr. Chestnut was appointed by the then American Presbyterian Board to China in 1893. She started a hospital in Lien-chou, Kwangsi, the province adjoining Hongkong. She lived on $1.50 a month so that the rest of her salary could be used to buy bricks. Her Board learned what she was spending on bricks and insisted on repaying her. She refused the sum offered, saying, "It will spoil all my fun."

While the building was under construction, she performed surgery in her bathroom. One operation involved the amputation of a coolie's leg. The surgery was successful, except that the flaps of skin did not grow together. Eventually this problem was solved and the man was able to walk with crutches. Someone noticed that Dr. Chestnut was limping. When asked why, she responded, "Oh, it's nothing." One of the nurses revealed the truth. The doctor had taken skin from her own leg for immediate transplant to the one whom nurses called "a good-for-nothing coolie," using only a local anesthetic.

When the Boxer uprising began Dr. Chestnut was one of the last missionaries to leave. She returned the following spring. On October 28, 1905, she and other missionaries were busy at the hospital when an anti-foreign mob attacked. She slipped out to ask for protection from Chinese authorities, and might have escaped had she not returned to help her fellow-workers. Her last act was to tear strips from her dress to bandage a wound in the forehead of a boy in the crowd. She was killed along with Rev. and Mrs. John Peale and two other missionaries.

Martyrs during the Revolution

In the decade after the Boxer defeat China wobbled chaotically toward Revolution. The medieval Manchu dynasty was dying. New leaders were rising and demanding a democratic form of government built on ideals they had learned from western missionaries. One revolutionary leader, Huang Hsing, declared, "To Christianity more than to any other single cause is owed our revolution." Yet in the turbulence of the fighting that culminated in the establishment of the Chinese Republic in 1911 missionaries were among those who suffered the most from bandits and mobs.

One of the first to die was Miss Christine Villadsen of the Scandinavian Alliance Mission. She was killed by bandits while trying to protect Chinese Christians at Shao-shui.

Ironically, supporters of the old Manchu dynasty sought refuge with missionaries in many cities. At Taiyuan, Shansi, the daughter of the Boxer governor who had ordered the murder of missionaries there in 1900, was given protection by British Baptists.

It was well known that many leaders of the Revolution had been educated in mission schools. Yet extreme elements in some areas of China were determined to vanquish foreigners, including missionaries, along with the Manchus.

The ancient city of Sian, southwest of Taiyuan, was the old capital of the Chinese Empire and had been a center of Manchu power. CIM missionaries had been twice driven out before Scandinavian Alliance missionaries located there. The work grew, churches were started, and a boarding school for children of the mission was built in a south suburb, beyond the wall of the city.

The missionaries knew that the anti-Manchu and antiforeign Ancient Society of Elder Brothers had hundreds of secret members in Sian. Though they were assured by national revolutionary leaders that they would be protected, E.R. Beckman, director of the school, and W.T. Vatne, a young teacher, were worried. When they discussed their situation, Beckman's oldest daughter Selma overheard and cried, "Let's go home."

Rumors of an impending attack spread throughout the area in early October, 1911. In this same month the churches in Sian were stirred by a remarkable revival. A young evangelist prophesied, "There are many evil men in this city, and something terrible will happen. Pray earnestly to the Lord."

On Sunday, October 22, Beckman was conducting services in a south suburb when he heard a military command and the sound of running feet. A messenger brought a note from his wife, imploring, "Hurry home." Beckman was stopped several times by soldiers, but finally reached the children's home.

That night the missionaries and the children crowded onto the veranda of the second floor. They could see pillars of fire in the distance—the wall of Sian was under attack.

Around midnight a mob massed at the gate in the high stone wall that protected the mission school. While the residents watched, soldiers torched the gate. They would be inside in a matter of minutes.

Beckman and Vatne got a rope to help the children over the back wall. Vatne went first, then Beckman helped his oldest daughter Selma over. The director had just put another child on top of the wall when shots rang out and his daughter screamed. Unable to help Vatne and Selma, he tried digging a hole in the wall at another spot. Then he heard shouts and timbers falling. The mob was through the gate.

Beckman, his wife Ida, and the six remaining children took shelter in a room of a small outbuilding. They could hear people running about and could smell smoke from more fires. "Find the foreigners! Kill them!" the intruders were shouting.

Mrs. Beckman tenderly took her youngest daughter, four-year-old Thyra, from her husband. She kissed the child and whispered, "I must say goodbye to you, my darling." Then she handed her back to her father.

Moments later their hiding place was discovered. They all dashed out, trying to run through the crowd milling around the yard. Beckman, carrying little Thyra, became separated from his wife and the others. Oblivious to blows from the fanatics who saw him, he rushed through the gate and ran into a grove of trees on the south bank of a large pond. Hearing voices behind him, he jumped in and waded to the middle of the pond where he and his child huddled in the thick vegetation which had grown out of the shallow water.

For the next three or four hours he remained there with his daughter in his arms. The little girl never uttered a sound. Finally the voices ceased and he saw flickering torches disappearing in the distance.

The morning star appeared. He feared that with the coming of day the mob would be back to search the pond. Holding little Thyra tightly, he cautiously waded to the north bank and crept through some bushes. Skirting a military camp, they reached a mission station hours later. Father and daughter were numb and exhausted, but otherwise in good health.

He was told that his wife, his middle daughter, and four other children had been killed while trying to break through the mob. But what of the teacher and Selma? Three days later he learned they had escaped and taken shelter with a Chinese family. Fanatics discovered them and a mob gathered demanding that they be given up. They tried to run and were slashed and beaten to death.

Revolutionary leaders made profuse apologies when told about the tragedy. This did little to console the grieving four-year-old. "Your momma and sisters and the others are with Jesus" Mr. Beckman kept assuring. Finally she asked, "Are they with *our* Jesus?" He nodded. "Then I will see them again."

Beckman took his daughter to Sweden for rest. There she developed diphtheria and hovered close to death. He and other Christians prayed and miraculously, she lived. Years later she married a missionary and served in China. She now lives in retirement in Woodstock, Illinois, awaiting the time when she will see her loved ones again.

Tragedies in the Twenties

The political future of China was decided in the 1920's. World War I weakened the European powers. Fueled by biblical ideas of freedom, China's new leaders began pressing for release from the foreign treaties that had milked the nation's resources for decades. Britain and the United States, which had the most missionaries in China, refused to give up the special privileges which were so profitable. Resentment flared against citizens of these countries living in China. Not since the time of the Boxers were missionaries in such great danger.

New philosophies and theologies from the West also helped to erode Chinese confidence in Christianity. A new wave of so-called missionaries from mainline Protestant denominations came teaching evolution and a non-supernatural view of the Bible. Methodist, Presbyterian, Congregationalist, and Northern Baptist schools were especially hard hit. Bertrand Russell came from England preaching atheism and socialism. Destructive books brought by such teachers further undermined orthodox Christianity. The Chinese intelligentsia who had been schooled by orthodox evangelical missionaries were thus softened for the advent of Marxism.

The crucial year was 1923. The United States and Britain again refused to give up their special rights in China. Sun Yat-sen, the Christian president, was facing a growing revolt in the south. Forth came the Soviet ambassador. His government, he pledged, would give up its treaty rights and help unify the country. Communism would not be established in China, he further promised.

On the last day of the year, President Sun announced, "We no longer look to the Western Powers. Our faces are turned toward Russia." The door was open for Communist agitation and infiltration that would inflame feelings against "imperialists" (missionaries and other western nationals) and their "running dogs" (Chinese Christians and employees of westerners).

Martyrs to Bandits and Kidnappers

Disorders and rebellions continued. In June, 1920, William A. Reimert, a missionary educator, was murdered by bandit soldiers. In December, 1921, the C&MA's W.H. Oldfields was kidnapped by brigands in Kwangsi Province. In 1922 Dr. Howard Taylor and four other CIM missionaries were seized by bandit soldiers, but were subsequently released. In August, 1923, F.J. Watts and E.A. Whiteside of the English Church Missionary Society were murdered by robbers in Szechwan Province. A few months later four American Lutheran missionaries were captured in Hupeh Province, and one, B.A. Hoff, died of injuries after his release. In 1924 George D. Byers, an American Presbyterian, was killed by bandits in Hainan Province. A few months later the anti-foreign Red Lantern Society murdered Mrs. Sible, a Canadian Methodist, at Ch'eng-tu. More kidnappings and murders followed, including the killing of several national Bible Society colporteurs.

A vast spiritual harvest paralleled the violence. For example, in Kweilin, capital of Kwangsi Province, thousands of new converts were baptized by Christian and Missionary Alliance missionaries. Three times the church sanctuary had to be enlarged. The foundation of the third building was laid during a period of near anarchy while bullets from battling military factions zinged over the construction site. C&MA

missionary Cunningham was supervising the work when hit by a fatal shot. His life and the lives of other missionaries and national church leaders were part of the price of the spiritual reaping.

The violence continued to escalate. Kidnappers no longer sent sliced ears as warnings, but killed their victims immediately if demands for ransom were not met. The antiforeign spirit, kept high by Communist agitation, was so strong that local military and civil authorities often looked the other way when attacks were made on missionaries and even on Chinese Christians.

The Blood Keeps Flowing

President Sun Yat-sen died in 1925. His party split apart, factions fighting among themselves. China became even less safe. Six more missionaries died, among them the beloved Bishop Cassels. Before his death he had written, "We came in the steps of Him who was despised and rejected of men. Perhaps this is one of the lessons we have to learn at a time when extraordinary and bitter hatred is being stirred up against us."

In 1926 the British Navy, in a show of force, sailed up the Yangtze Gorges and bombarded the populous city of Wan-hsien. Hundreds of Chinese were killed. Anti-foreign passions flamed so high that hundreds of Chinese churches severed relations with foreign mission boards. Marshall Feng, the famed Christian general, went to Moscow to study communism.

The year 1927 was the worst since the Boxer violence in 1900. Mission hospitals and schools had to be closed in the interior of China. Missionaries were ordered to evacuate to the coast or return home. In that year the Protestant force dropped from sixty-five hundred to four thousand.

Crossing deserts and high mountains, missionaries were again easy prey for bandits and undisciplined troops. In one incident bandits attacked three CIM American missionaries, Mr. and Mrs. Morris Slichter, their two children, and Miss May Craig. They were traveling under military guard to a railway station in Yunnan Province. When the bandits opened fire, the guards fled leaving the missionaries unprotected in a rice field. Heedless of cries for mercy, one bandit fired at Mrs. Slichter who was holding her three-year-old daughter Ruth in her arms. The bullet passed through the child's head and ripped a gash across the mother's left wrist. Another robber stabbed Mr. Slichter in the back. He fell dead without a sound. These bandits raced on in pursuit of the guards. Others coming up behind paused only to rob Mr. Slichter's body and snatch Mrs. Slichter and Miss Craig's glasses before running on.

When the battle was over, the robbers returned and carried the dead and living off to their village. Little Ruth had died a few minutes after being hit. Eight days later Chinese soldiers attacked the village. The robbers, dragging their three captives, scattered into the hills under a hail of bullets. At daybreak the bandits regrouped and decided to leave Miss Craig with a letter to the soldiers warning that if they continued to follow, Mrs. Slichter and her son would be killed. The soldiers called off the chase, but returned to the village and seized the bandit leader's family as a ransom for the release of the two Americans. The exchange was made.

In remote Kansu Province Dr. George King, director of the Borden Memorial Hospital, was the only physician for a thousand miles. Young Bill Borden, heir to a fortune and a scholar-athlete graduate of both Princeton and Yale, had died in Egypt while studying Arabic in preparation for missionary service among the Moslems of northwest China. One quarter of his estate had been left to the CIM and had been used to build the hospital.

Dr. King did not want to leave his post, but since he was a strong swimmer and proficient in Chinese, his help was needed in evacuating thirty-seven missionaries and twelve children by goatskin rafts down the Yellow River. They were attacked by bandits along one remote stretch. Fortunately, the current was strong enough to allow them to escape. Then a few miles down the river they became stuck on a sand bar. Twelve hours in the water, tugging at the rafts, sapped the doctor's strength. When all but one of the rafts had been freed, he slipped into a nasty current. "Can you make it?" someone called. "I don't know," he replied, and slipped under, never to be seen again.

Chinese Christians Were Not Spared

For every missionary who died directly or indirectly because of the violence, at least ten Chinese Christians lost their lives. One was Y.C. Liu, a promising scholarly young preacher in Szechwan Province. He was on his way to his ordination ceremony in a CIM–related church when kidnapped by bandits. His body was later found in the woods. Another Chinese Christian from the same area was the former incense-maker, Ho. After hearing the gospel, Ho had invited missionary C.M. Tan and his Christian brother-in-law to the destruction of his idols. A man of few words, he became known for his warm smile and willingness to tackle any task in the church. While on a trip to sell cloth, he was stopped by brigands, robbed, and killed. Left to mourn were his wife and three young children.

Besides the bandit peril, Chinese Christians continued to be targets of anti-foreign and anti-Christian societies. Traveling Bible and book salesmen were especially in danger. One was seized in Kiangsi Province, his books were confiscated, and his hands tied. He was ordered to run through the streets, calling out, "I am also an imperialist, a slavish dog of the foreigners." Instead he proclaimed at the top of his lungs, "I am a slave of Jesus Christ!" They did not kill him on the spot, but threatened to do so if he ever dared sell another Christian book. How long he lived after this is not known. Another Chinese Christian in Yonanchow, Hunan Province, was grabbed by Communists and charged with being a "running dog of imperialists" for disseminating the teachings of Jesus. When told he was worthy of death, he begged the opportunity to pray. A Communist instantly struck off his hand. "Lord Jesus, receive my spirt," the Christian shouted in a loud voice. A second blow with the sword and he was dead.

The Nationalist armies now pushed north and conquered the upper Yangtze Valley. With the fall of Nanking on March 27 many foreigners, including missionaries, were murdered. Many others escaped. Pearl S. Buck, daughter of missionaries and later to become a world-renowned novelist, hid in a peasant hut. A Southern Presbyterian doctor was pushed into a hospital coalbin by his loyal staff. After the danger had passed, he crawled out, sooty but safe.

The Red Peril

Chiang Kai-shek purged the Communists from his armies and reversed Sun's policy of friendship with Russia. In 1928 the long civil war began between Chiang's Nationalist armies and the Communists under Mao Tse-tung. Vastly outnumbered by Nationalist troops, the Communist armies retreated to the far northwest. But infiltrators and guerrillas remained hidden in the dense population.

Undaunted, the CIM called for two hundred new workers in 1929 to serve in dangerous areas. "It will involve the most tremendous conflict [with Satan] which we have ever undertaken," said the CIM director. Within the next few months eight more missionaries were killed, thirty captured and held for ransom, and twenty of thirty-two CIM stations looted. The price of serving in China remained high. In 1930 three missionaries of the Finnish Free Mission Society, Misses Cajander, Ingman and Hedengren were killed by Communist outlaws. Altogether, during 1930, the Communists killed an estimated one hundred fifty thousand Chinese in Kiangsi Province and burned one hundred thousand homes. One and a half million Chinese fled the province in fear.

When Chiang Kai-shek declared himself a Christian the next year, missionaries and Chinese church leaders became direct targets for Communist hostility. Propagandists nailed up posters announcing such charges as, "The church is the headquarters of murderers and incendiaries," "The missionaries have love in their mouths and hate in their hearts," and "Christians are traitors to China." Other posters urged Chinese, "Drive out these missionaries who are making slaves of us." To the testimony of one CIM missionary in Kiangsi Province that he was not afraid to die because "I know I will go to Heaven," a Communist answered, "Let him go to Heaven. We will have one less missionary in China to cheat the people."

Missionaries urgently warned their home offices and government officials in western countries of the Communist threat to China. But the West paid no heed and continued to enforce profitable trade concession treaties with China.

Moslem Marauders

The decade of the thirties began with terrible famines and plagues added to Communist guerrilla activities and other rebellions in many cities. In Minchow, Kansu, the Assemblies of God lost one hundred fifty school children out of five hundred students in a plague. Next, bandits attacked the town, seizing citizens by force and torturing them until they gave up their valuables. Hundreds were burned and beaten.

Many Christians among them died. The bandits had hardly left when thirty thousand rebellious Moslems marched in and took control. Their leader made his headquarters in the front yard of the Assemblies mission house. The Moslems looted, burned, raped and killed at will for eighteen days. When missionary W.W. Simpson tried to have a worship service, a brute on the Moslem General's staff seated himself on the platform. As Simpson spoke about the coming of Christ into the world, the Moslem made motions with his sword of cutting off the missionary's head. Surprisingly, the missionary was spared.

The brutalities were even worse in Tsinchow, Kansu Province. A Moslem army captured the town in May, killed twenty-seven hundred natives in three days, took over a thousand young women captive, and turned the CIM girls' school into horse stalls.

Afraid of What?

In October, 1931, widower Jack Vinson, a beloved Southern Presbyterian missionary, was captured by bandits while visiting rural churches in Kiangsu Province. A government force, loyal to Chiang, pursued the kidnappers and surrounded them in a small town. The bandits offered the missionary freedom if he would persuade the force to withdraw. Vinson agreed only if they would release other captives. The bandits refused and tried to shoot their way out. In the melee many bandits were killed, and the survivors fled with Vinson. However, the missionary could not run because of recent surgery. One bandit shot him, then another ran up and cut off his head.

The daughter of a Chinese pastor was among those rescued by government troops. She recalled having heard a bandit tell him, "I'm going to kill you. Aren't you afraid?" She said Vinson had replied simply, "Kill me, if you wish. I will go straight to God."

Jack Vinson was the first Southern Presbyterian martyr in China. A colleague, E.H. Hamilton, was inspired by his courage to write a poem that was widely printed and became an encouragement to other missionaries and Chinese believers in constant danger.

> Afraid? Of What?
> To feel the spirit's glad release?
> To pass from pain to perfect peace,

The strife and strain of life to cease?
Afraid—of that?

Afraid? Of What?
Afraid to see the Savior's face
To hear His welcome, and to trace
The glory gleam from wounds of grace?
Afraid—of that?

Afraid? Of What?
A flash, a crash, a pierced heart;
Darkness, light, O Heaven's art!
A wound of His a counterpart!
Afraid—of that?

Afraid? Of What?
To do by death what life could not—
Baptize with blood a stony plot,
Till souls shall blossom from the spot?
Afraid—of that?

Victory Day for the Stams

John and Betty Stam, new CIM missionaries in hazardous Anhwei Province were among those strengthened by "Afraid? Of What?" They had met at CIM student prayer meetings at Moody. Betty, a gifted poet, had been raised in China of Presbyterian missionary parents and felt God's call to return there. John, of Dutch immigrant ancestry from New Jersey, was also drawn to the land where, as he said, "a million a month pass into Christless graves."

At that time the CIM was calling for a vanguard of single men to serve in dangerous Communist-infested areas. Even though this could mean not marrying for several years, if at all, John was willing to go. Chosen to give the Class Address for the Moody Class of '32, he challenged,

> Shall we beat a retreat, and turn back from our high calling in Christ Jesus; or dare we advance at God's command in face of the impossible? ... Let us remind ourselves that the Great Commission was never qualified by clauses calling for advance only if funds were plentiful and no hardship or self-denial involved. On the contrary, we are told to expect tribulation and even persecution, but with it victory in Christ.

Since Betty was a year ahead of John in school, she went to

China first. Assigned to Anhwei Province, she was delayed in Shanghai when the veteran CIM missionary in Anhwei, H.S. Ferguson, was captured by bandits and all the women missionaries had to leave. Ferguson was never seen alive again.

So she was in Shanghai when John arrived and after a year they were given permission by the CIM director to be married. "Truly, God seems to go out of His way to make His children happy," John wrote his parents after the wedding. They were even happier when Helen Priscilla was born in September, 1934, in a Methodist hospital far up the Yangtze River.

Communist activity was said to have subsided in Anhwei Province, and they were assigned to do evangelistic work in the town of Ching-te. The district magistrate assured, "There is no danger of Communists here. I will guarantee your safety."

A few weeks later Communists did attack and the magistrate was one of the first to flee. The Reds were quick to go to the Stams'. Betty served them tea and cakes while John tried to explain their peaceful intentions. When they finished their tea, the visitors politely said, "You will go with us."

At the direction of his captors, John wrote CIM that the kidnappers wanted $20,000 ransom. "The Lord bless and guide you, and as for us, may God be glorified whether by life or by death." He told the Communists, "I do not expect the ransom to be paid."

The Reds abandoned Ching-te, taking their captives with them. On the trail they discussed killing the baby to save trouble. An old farmer protested, "The little one has done nothing worthy of death." "Then you will die for her," the leader retorted. "I am willing," said the farmer. He was killed on the spot.

They stopped in the town of Miao-shou and ordered John to send another letter demanding the ransom. The postmaster recognized him and asked, "Where are you going?" "We don't know where they're going," John replied, "but we are going to heaven."

A short time later they were painfully bound, stripped of their outer garments, and quartered in a house. The next morning, still bound, they were marched through the town. As they moved along, the Communists shouted ridicule and hate slogans and called the people to the execution.

The procession stopped in a pine grove at the top of a hill. Suddenly the town physician, Dr. Wang, a Christian, ran to the prisoners and pleaded for their lives. He was dragged away to be killed.

John was asking mercy for the doctor when ordered to kneel. The executioner swung his sword and the young missionary was gone. Betty quivered momentarily, then fell beside him. Another swing and they were together with God.

The "Miracle Baby"

The next day a Chinese evangelist named Lo arrived. The Communist soldiers had left, but the townspeople were too terrified of Communist spies to talk. Finally an old woman pointed to a vacant house and whispered, "The foreign baby is still alive." Lo found the baby lying warm and snug on a bed and took her to his wife. Then they recovered the bodies of the parents and lovingly wrapped them in white cotton for burial.

The bravery of the evangelist and his wife shamed the townspeople and they gathered to hear his funeral sermon.

> You have seen these wounded bodies, and you pity our friends for their suffering and death. But you should know that they are children of God. Their spirits are unharmed, and are at this moment in the presence of their Heavenly Father. They came to China and to Miao-shou, not for themselves but for you, to tell you about the great love of God, that you might believe in the Lord Jesus and be eternally saved. You have heard their message. Remember, it is true. Their death proves it so. Do not forget what they told you — repent, and believe the Gospel.

After the burial Evangelist and Mrs. Lo tenderly carried little Priscilla in a rice basket a hundred miles through dangerous mountains to the home of another CIM missionary, George Birch. Along the road they had asked Chinese mothers to nurse the child. Birch promised to care for her until his wife returned. Tucked away in the baby's clothing was ten dollars hidden by the mother for food.

When Mrs. Birch arrived, the couple arranged for the tiny orphan to be taken to its mother's parents, Dr. and Mrs. Charles Scott, at their Presbyterian station in Chi-nan, Shantung Province. Dr. Scott said of his daughter and son-in-law: "They have not died in vain. The blood of the martyrs is still the seed of the church. If we could hear our beloved children speak, we know from their convictions that they would praise God because He counted them worthy to suffer for the sake of Christ."

The report of the Stams' martyrdom and the survival of the "miracle baby," as Priscilla was called, was widely publicized in the United States and Britain. Hundreds of letters came to the parents of the young couple and their mission. Many contained large gifts. Some writers volunteered to go as replacements. At Moody and at Wilson College, where Betty had also attended, there were student prayer meetings. A biography was published and quickly ran through nine printings. Noting the impact, a CIM missionary in China wrote Betty's parents, "A life which had the longest span of years might not have been able to do one-hundredth of the work for Christ which they have done in a day."

Martyrs to Disease

More missionaries died in China from dread diseases than from violence. The C&MA, for example, lost ten missionaries to smallpox, typhus, dysentery and malaria from 1900-24, while losing only two workers to afflictions common in the homeland. The larger CIM mission lost many more to dread diseases. Missionary doctors were most vulnerable to diseases such as smallpox, cholera and typhus because they were often involved in fighting epidemics.

Dr. Arthur Jackson was a living legend in Manchuria where he was director of a Presbyterian hospital. When the bubonic plague struck, he worked day and night trying to save as many lives as possible. In the midst of the epidemic he caught the plague from patients and died. Thousands attended a memorial service where the viceroy, not a Christian himself, gave the eulogy. "The Chinese government has lost a man who gave his life in his desire to help," he said. Then he followed Chinese custom and addressed a prayer to the departed missionary doctor.

> O spirit of Dr. Jackson, we pray you to intercede for the twenty million people of Manchuria and ask the Lord of Heaven to take away this pestilence, so that we may once more lay our heads in peace upon our pillows. In life you were brave, now you are an exalted spirit. Noble spirit, who sacrificed your life for us, help us still, and look down in kindness upon us all.

Another killer disease was typhus fever, marked by eruption of red spots, cerebral disorders and extreme prostration. Without treatment, victims usually died or were left with permanent brain damage. Typhus claimed two of China's most renowned medical missionaries.

Dr. Gaynor of the Quaker Friends' Mission provided a hospital and refuge in Nanking for officials and relatives from the deposed Manchu dynasty. In 1912 the Quaker physician contracted the disease from patients and died.

Dr. Whitfield Guinness, chief of the CIM hospital at Kaifeng, caught typhus while treating Chinese soldiers during the chaotic year of 1927. He was critically ill when anti-foreign mobs began forming to attack the hospital. Friends carried him to the railway station and shoved his bed into a crowded boxcar for evacuation to Peking. Two nights in the jolting, swaying, unventilated car proved too much. He died shortly after reaching the capital.

Many other missionaries were struck down by diseases they would not have contracted at home. The Scandinavian Alliance Mission lost four workers in the year 1930 alone. One of the four, Mary Anderson, had worked alone in a dangerous bandit-infested area for thirty-four years. But while the bandits respected her, the dread fever did not.

The multi-talented J.O. Fraser—preacher, linguist, musician, and engineer—came to Yunnan Province in 1910 and mastered the difficult Lisu language. Developing his own "Fraser Script," he devoted himself to translating Scripture into the tribal dialect. In 1916 the Lisu began turning from their demon worship to Christ in large numbers. Sixty thousand were baptized in a two year period. The Lisu church continued to grow and became one of the largest tribal Christian bodies in the world. Then in 1937, in the peak of life, the "apostle to the Lisus" came down with malignant malaria while on a trip in the mountains and died.

Shine On, Lottie Moon
Famine, the result of floods and drought, was the greatest destroyer of all. The loss of life in China in the first third of the twentieth century would have been infinitely greater without emergency relief programs funded by Christians in the United States and Britain and administered by missionaries. In 1906 one Christian periodical, *Christian Herald*, raised and forwarded $450,000 in gold. Upwards of two mil-

lion lives were saved. Many impressed Chinese came to the missionaries, asking, "Tell us about your religion."

Too often the money was not available from home, and missionaries were helpless to prevent mass starvation. They had only their own small salaries for purchasing food. Some hastened their own deaths by going without.

The most celebrated martyr to hunger was Lottie Moon, a household name among Southern Baptists today. Each Christmas Southern Baptist women in thirty-five thousand American churches gather an offering in Miss Moon's name for foreign missions.

Born and reared in Virginia Baptist aristocracy, Lottie Moon was self-willed and rebellious through most of college. Surrender to Christ was not easy. Of her conversion she said, "I went to the service to scoff, and returned to my room to pray all night."

Her younger sister Edmonia went to China first. Charlotte went to Cartersville, Georgia, to teach. There she sought out destitute families for whom she bought clothing from her own purse. One morning the pastor spoke on the text, "Lift up your eyes, and look on the fields; for they are white already to harvest." At the close of the sermon the young teacher walked down the aisle and declared, "I have long known God wanted me in China. I am now ready to go."

She joined Edmonia in 1873 at Tengchow in northern Shantung Province. Edmonia was later compelled to leave China permanently because of poor health. Charlotte gave herself without reserve to her teaching and evangelistic work and to pleading for new workers from the homeland. She sometimes struck sparks in letters to her Board. "It is odd that a million Baptists of the South can furnish only three men for all China," she wrote once. "Odd that with five hundred preachers in the state of Virginia we must rely on a Presbyterian minister to fill a Baptist pulpit [here]. I wonder how these things look in heaven. They certainly look very queer in China—but the Baptists are a great people, as we never tire of saying in our associations and conventions, and possibly our way of doing things is best!"

When more men finally were appointed, the decision was made that women should not share policy making with them. Miss Moon promptly submitted her resignation over the issue and officials backed down.

In 1887 she was preparing to leave for furlough when two Chinese men arrived. They had walked 115 miles to seek a teacher. There was no one else to send, so she went. This was the year when she suggested that Southern Baptist women designate a week of prayer and offerings for missions the week before Christmas. "I wonder how many of us really believe that it is more blessed to give than to receive," she challenged.

She was now facing persecution and hatred for being a foreigner. Frequently she was called "Devil Old Woman." After receiving a death threat, she underlined this sentence in her copy of *Imitation of Christ:* "Thou oughtest so to order thyself in all thy thoughts and actions, as if today thou wert to die."

She survived through most of the Boxer Rebellion before agreeing to evacuate to Japan for a few months. In 1911 came the Revolution, followed by famine. The Chinese churches did all they could. Miss Moon regularly gave a large part of her salary. She wrote to the Southern Baptist Foreign Mission Board again and again. Each time the reply was negative. The Board was heavily in debt and could hardly pay missionary salaries. Not one cent had been budgeted for famine relief.

She wrote a nephew, begging him to speak with his pastor about a local church offering. She told of mothers eager to give their children away and warned that "unless help comes from one to three million must perish from hunger. One penny a day up to the next harvest will save a life. How can we bear to sit down to our bountiful tables and know of such things and not bestir."

The famine worsened. Her appeals to the homeland continued to receive no response. She drew out the last of her savings from a bank in Shanghai to send to relief workers. "I pray that no missionary will ever be as lonely as I have been," she wrote in her bank book.

Fellow missionaries began noticing that she was behaving strangely and appeared befuddled. They sent for a doctor. One look told him she was starving to death. Indeed she had vowed to eat no more so long as her Chinese friends were starving.

Gentle hands gave her nourishment and put her on a ship for home with a missionary nurse escort. Enroute, the ship stopped at Kobe, Japan. There on Christmas Eve night,

1912, she lapsed into unconsciousness. The nurse saw her lips move and bent to catch the name of a Chinese friend. Her frail, thin, almost transparent hands were moving, clasping and unclasping in the Chinese fashion of greeting. She was saying goodbye to old friends. Or was she saying hello? Finally her hands grew still, her breathing stopped, and she was in the heavenly company.

After cremation (required by Japanese law) her ashes were delivered to Virginia and buried under whispering pines. At the head of her grave her family placed a marble stone with the inscription:
LOTTIE MOON 1840–1912
FORTY YEARS A MISSIONARY OF THE SOUTHERN BAPTIST CONVENTION IN CHINA
"FAITHFUL UNTO DEATH"
Her home church hired an artisan to design the figure of a beautiful woman in graceful, flowing garments, walking through a field of lilies, one hand clasping the Word of God to her heart, the other holding high a blazing torch. On this he inscribed in gold lettering:
GO YE, THEREFORE, AND TEACH ALL NATIONS
Back in China her Christian friends erected their own memorial stone:
A MONUMENT TO BEQUEATH THE LOVE OF
MISS LOTTIE MOON
AN AMERICAN MISSIONARY
THE CHINESE CHURCH REMEMBERS FOREVER
But her greatest memorials have been the numbers of young Christians who have been challenged by her life and the annual week-of-prayer-offerings taken in thirty-five thousand Southern Baptist churches every year for foreign missions. In 1976 the collection amounted to almost thirty million dollars.

Martyrs in War
A new and dangerous period of world history had begun in the thirties. China was at center stage and again the Chinese church and Christian missionaries were caught in the violent vortex. Many heralds of the cross gave their lives.

In 1930 the Shinto zealot Baron Tanaka became prime minister of Japan. Tanaka reasserted *hakko-ichiu*—"the whole world under one roof." Japan's destiny, he vowed, was to bring the world under the rule of Shintoism, as personified by the Japanese emperor, worshiped as the Imperial incarnation of the Sun Goddess.

China was then reeling from epidemics, famines, communist terror and factional wars. Taking advantage of the weakness of Japan's long-time traditional enemy, Baron Tanaka and other war lords seized two northern provinces and demanded that China give independence to five other northern provinces. To buy time in his fight against the Communists, Chiang agreed. Then the Communists scored a dramatic coup. They kidnapped Chiang and forced him to sign a truce.

The Japanese launched an all-out attack in 1937 and by 1939 had conquered most of populous eastern China. American missionaries warned their homeland of Japan's global intention. But the United States refused to intervene and even continued selling war material to Japan which was used to bomb innocent civilians.

During the Boxer uprising and the other anti-foreign rebellions that had followed, it had not been safe for missionaries to be on the street. The situation was now reversed. Foreigners were given safe conduct, for Japan did not want to provoke intervention from abroad.

Undisciplined soldiers looted, raped and killed as they desired. Thousands of Chinese girls were gang raped, then killed for sport. Traveling missionaries sometimes came across trembling Chinese men sitting by the roadside. Their story was always the same: Japanese soldiers had driven them from their homes, keeping behind their wives and daughters. The only safe place was with foreigners. When soldiers were about, mission schools, hospitals and homes were jammed with Chinese women and girls.

Both Japanese and Communists persecuted Christians, although the Japanese were careful about disturbing a church when missionaries were around. Apart from missionaries, Chinese church leaders were fair game. In Shansi Province thirteen Christian leaders were rounded up at one time and shot. In mountainous tribal areas Communist guerrillas continued killing Christians as they had before the Japanese occupation.

Patriotic Chinese Christian leaders refused to kowtow to the invaders. One of the most notable was Dr. Herman Liu, the first Chinese president of the Baptist University of

Shanghai, who held the Ph.D. degree from Columbia University. He headed up refugee work in occupied Shanghai.

The Japanese put him on their blacklist. Many attempts were made on his life. He was sent flowers with notes of warning. The gate leading to his home was dynamited. Poisoned fruit was delivered to his home—he discovered the poison just in time.

Friends begged him to flee, but he refused, declaring, "I will remain as the Lord can use me here. I will not desert."

On the morning of April 8, 1938, Japanese soldiers shot him to death in front of his home, where he was waiting with his young son for a bus to take him to his office. His friends tearfully held his funeral while a crowd of five thousand waited outside the church, unable to get in. On a cross over his grave was inscribed:

HERMAN LIU, CHRISTIAN MARTYR AND PATRIOT.

Still the Chinese church was unbent. One woman told CIM missionaries: "My house has been burned twice and nothing is left. Four of six relatives there are dead, including my brother who was branded with a hot iron. My daughter-in-law was shot before my eyes and my only grandson has died from exposure. But I will not let go of Jesus Christ."

Missionary work in China became more hazardous after Pearl Harbor. In areas already under control hundreds were seized and placed in internment camps. Missionaries in unoccupied areas of China had to evacuate as Japanese armies moved closer. Many got out just in the nick of time by hastily arranged five-hundred-mile flights by the U. S. Air Transport Command over the dangerous Himalayan "Hump" to Burma. There were numerous accidents. In 1944 the CIM alone lost three missionaries in plane crashes.

During this second phase of the war, thousands of Chinese Christians perished or lost all their property. In some regions entire church congregations vanished. Nevertheless, between 1937 and 1945, evangelicals in China increased from six hundred thousand to seven hundred fifty thousand.

The Real John Birch

John Birch is one of the most remarkable martyrs of this period. Unfortunately, his service to China has been all but forgotten in the controversy over the political organization named after him.

Born in India of missionary parents, Birch graduated at the head of his high school, college and seminary classes. He went to Hangchow in 1940 under the World Fundamentalist Baptist Missionary Fellowship and immediately demonstrated an unusual proficiency in learning the language and adapting to the culture. Within a year he was slipping through Japanese occupation lines and preaching in villages where missionaries had not dared to go since the war began.

After Pearl Harbor the Japanese ordered his arrest. But he had fled to Shang-jao in Kiangsi Province from which he and four Chinese preachers sustained national churches for several months. Because Shang-jao was still in "free" territory, he became a conduit for American funds sent to missionaries stranded in Shanghai.

As the war progressed, he became a one-man rescue unit, helping missionaries and Chinese preachers evacuate before advancing Japanese. In one operation called "Harvey's Restaurant" he arranged for sixty missionaries and children to be flown out to safety. In another he rescued Colonel James Doolittle, the most celebrated American flier shot down during the war.

He asked to join the American Military Mission as a chaplain. Instead he was commissioned a captain in intelligence and told he could preach all he wanted. He became a legend. He was the only American who had the complete trust of the Chinese Army and could go anywhere. His commander Colonel Wilfred Smith said later, "John influenced more as a military officer than he did as a missionary."

But he never saw himself as anything but a missionary. "I'm just making tents," he wrote his father. "When the war is over, I'll be ready to welcome the others back."

His announced intention to remain in China after the war may have led to his death. He was sent to convince hold-out pockets of Japanese in north China that the war was over. Communists, under the guise of "agrarian reformers," were then entrenched in north China, awaiting the opportunity to resume their war of conquest. Birch and his team were intercepted by a column of Chinese who were not supposed to be there. "Let us take you to our commander," they offered. Warned by his lieutenant that he might be walking into a trap, Birch decided to go. "It doesn't make any difference what happens to me," he said, "but it is of utmost importance that my country learn now whether these people are friend or foe." His body was found the next day, punctured and slashed by bayonets.

Chinese friends tenderly wrapped his body in white silk. He was buried in a Chinese coffin with full military honors, several missionaries and Chinese pastors looking on. On his stone they placed the inscription:
HE DIED FOR RIGHTEOUSNESS.
Only the barest details of his death were released to his family by the State Department. In the amoral game of diplomacy Communists were never blamed. There were at the time Red sympathizers ensconsed in high places in the United States government. It was also later disclosed that the decisive United States atomic bombing mission had been carried out with the aid of essential weather bulletins from Mao Tse-tung's Communists in north China.

Why was John Birch killed? The best speculation is that the Chinese Reds did not want him around as a missionary after the war.

Martyrs of Red China

The West was blind to the Red tide washing across China. But the old China hands who returned to their mission posts soon saw the handwriting on the wall. The Soviets had declared war on Japan in the closing days of the war—to grab Manchuria, some thought. The Chinese Marxists had helped the Americans defeat the Japanese in China and gained valuable experience in guerrilla warfare. All during the war they had been subverting and plotting to take over the government.

Meanwhile, the opportunities for evangelism seemed never greater. Most churches had either held their own or actually grown during the years of war and Japanese occupation. Missionaries and national church leaders began reopening hospitals and schools and launching evangelistic crusades.

The euphoria was short-lived as Communist propagandists began stirring up old hatreds against Americans. Communist armies launched new attacks. Banditry intensified, making travel as dangerous as ever.

In December, 1947, Evangelical Covenant Church missionaries at Hankow became concerned about their colleagues in Kingchow which was in imminent danger of being taken by the Communists. On January 7 Dr. Alexis Berg, Esther Nordlund and Martha Anderson left by transport truck to consult with their friends. Some of the passengers, worried about a bandit attack, had hired an armed guard.

About two in the afternoon as they were traveling through deserted hilly country, a shot rang out. The driver stopped immediately and one of the guards fired a shot to scare off any small group. More shouts and more firing— then about sixty armed men appeared. The guard fled.

The bandits advanced on the passengers and ordered them to get off the truck and to give up their valuables. The missionaries were also forced to give up their coats and shoes. Dr. Berg asked if he might keep his passport. At that one bandit cursed and slapped his face. The doctor handed the passport over. A passing bicyclist was stopped. When he hesitated to give anything up, the bandits shot him dead.

They then left by scrambling up a nearby hill. Part way up, four turned around and returned.

"Shall we kill these foreigners?" the leader asked. Then looking at Dr. Berg, he demanded, "Are you Americans?" When Dr. Berg did not reply, the bandit snarled, "Americans are the worst of all. They have done China much harm." Then he shot Dr. Berg through the head.

When the shot was fired, Miss Anderson burst into sobs. The bandit leader responded, "She must be a relative of his," and immediately shot her also. By this time some of the passengers were kneeling, pleading with the bandits to stop killing. The four consulted briefly among themselves, then turned toward Miss Nordlund. "Yes, you may kill me, too," she said. Then she was shot. None of the other passengers were killed.

The killers left. But the frightened passengers insisted that the driver take them on and leave the bodies by the roadside. The bodies were later recovered and taken to Kingchow. The missionaries there sorrowfully dressed the bodies and placed them in coffins. They were taken back to Hankow for a final service and buried in the International Cemetery among the graves of scores of other departed missionaries who had given their all for Christ in China.

The Communist armies kept advancing. By 1949 the conquest was all but complete. There was much hand wringing and finger pointing in the West. It was said "fuzzy" liberals and hidden Communists in the United States government had blinded the Americans until it was too late to rescue Chiang. There was less quibbling over other factors, such as corruption in the Nationalist government, runaway inflation and student unrest. Later even the liberals had to concede they had been duped while the Communists had followed their game plan to victory.

The Communists sought to destroy the old Confucius order of family loyalty and morality and level the social system. Millions were killed for nothing more than owning property and paying respect to parents. How many Christians died in the secret genocidal purges will never be known.

Not wanting to inflame world opinion, the new "People's Republic" pursued a more wily strategy against Christianity. First they got rid of most of the missionaries, not by execution but by cutting ties between East and West. They charged that Christianity as it existed was too closely tied to western imperialism and colonialism. Missionaries were suddenly without jobs, property and financial support. For example, the CIM, still the largest mission, had served in China eighty-five years. By 1953 it did not have a single worker in China nor a piece of furniture to call its own. The schools, hospitals and all properties of the CIM and other foreign missions were confiscated.

Taking a lesson from history, the CIM changed its name to Overseas Missionary Fellowship, began accepting Asian workers on a par with Westerners, established headquarters in Singapore, and began work in East Asian countries.

By 1950 only a scattering of missionaries remained in China. Some had welcomed communism as a partner to Christianity and were outright propagandists for the regime. The others were holdouts, determined to stay until they were forcibly removed, imprisoned or killed. Along with the Protestants were not a few Catholic diehards who died in prison.

The Communists had a step-by-step plan for dealing with the immovables: false accusations, planting of evidence, arrest, showcase trial, imprisonment, interrogations and torture until the victim signed a confession, then if life remained, release of the shattered mind and body to authorities in Hongkong.

Many faithful evangelists and pastors were arrested, never to be heard from again. One was Pastor Wang Shih-kuang, who was conducting a morning service at Ch'in-hsien in northwest China when Communists entered. The venerable preacher had apparently been expecting arrest. Raising his hand, he said simply, "This is God's service. Kindly remain at the back until we have finished." The Communists complied.

When the service was over and the soldiers came forward, Pastor Wang had only one last request. "Permit me to change clothes first." They understood. When a Chinese believes death is upon him, he wants to be dressed in his best garments. A few minutes later Pastor Wang reappeared, properly dressed, for his trip to jail. His fate was never known. The bodies of those who died in prison were usually released with the cause of death cited as disease, accident or suicide.

Indomitable Bill Wallace

The diabolical brutality of twisted Marxist minds is no better illustrated than in the treatment given a Baptist bachelor surgeon from Knoxville, Tennessee.

The quiet and devout Wallace joined the staff of Stout Memorial Hospital in Wuchow in 1935. A veteran missionary on board ship had told him that during the first half century of Protestant work in China, only one missionary had reached age forty. Wallace surpassed that by only three years. He steadfastly refused all marriage prospects. One hopeful said after a short acquaintance, "Marriage to Bill would be bigamy. He's married to his work."

The first incident occurred when he returned from language school to find the other missionaries had departed in fear of an advancing bandit army. He simply pulled the Chinese staff together and went to work. An American ship anchored in the nearby river. The captain sent an officer to remind the young surgeon that he could not be responsible for his safety even if he stayed overnight. "Tell your captain," Wallace said, "that he was not responsible for my coming here in the first place and he does not need to be responsible for my staying here."

The Japanese could not bomb him out during their war with China. He stubbornly remained during World War II until Wuchow officials decided the city must be evacuated.

Then he put the hospital on water by transferring staff and equipment to a barge. When enemy planes roared overhead, he had the tugboat captain pull the floating hospital into one of the many large caves along the riverbank.

After VJ Day he set up shop again in the old building at Wuchow and for four years operated in peace. Then the Communists took over. One by one his missionary colleagues had to leave. Finally only he and nurse Everly Hayes remained. Local Communists tried to impose a crippling tax. Wallace said he could not believe the new People's Republic would so handicap an institution of mercy. Local citizens rose up and demanded exemption. It was granted.

The Korean War was on and Communists in Wuchow mounted a "hate America" campaign. But the only "American dogs" and "imperialist wolves" remaining in the city were Dr. Wallace and Nurse Hayes, and Wallace was renowned as the finest surgeon in south China. The propaganda campaign fizzled.

One pre-dawn morning more than twenty Communist soldiers came to the hospital gate claiming to have a sick man. When the gate was opened, they rushed to the doctor's house. "We hide nothing," Wallace protested. "Our only work is healing the suffering and sick in the name of Jesus Christ."

A planted pistol was excuse enough to arrest and jail the doctor for espionage. From his cell Wallace preached to peasants brave enough to come within hearing.

At a mock trial his prosecutors waved a paper they said was his signed confession. What they had gotten from Wallace was only a brief, factual biographical summary. After he had signed it, they had typed in the confession. Citizen accusers were asked to come forward. To the prosecutor's ambarrassment, no one moved. No matter. At a prearranged signal, hired stooges stood to deliver false testimony.

The missionary doctor was convicted, sentenced to prison, then marched through the streets to the main prison. His hands were tied and he wore a placard bearing obscene charges. Along the way he was shoved by a guard, and he fell badly hurting his hand.

The next days were a nightmare of almost hourly interrogations accompanied by charges of medical incompetence, murdering and maiming Chinese, performing obscene operations, and immoral conduct with nurses. Once he was forced to pose holding a radio aerial for a picture to prove the spy conviction.

Near the end of one brutal day in February, 1951, one of the Catholic missionaries asked from a nearby cell how he was holding out. "Trusting in the Lord," came the weak reply. His prison mates often heard him crying out in agony. It was also learned later that he wrote short Scripture verses, affirmations of faith, and denials of guilt on pieces of paper which he stuck on his cell walls and repeated to prepare for the next grilling.

The questioning continued, the pressure unrelenting. He became delirious and lapsed into crying spells.

Perhaps in fear of punishment for not succeeding, his guards used long poles to jab him into unconsciousness. The next morning they ran along the cellblock yelling, "The doctor has hung himself." They showed the Catholic priests where he was hanging from a beam and asked them to sign a statement attesting to his suicide. They would only state that they found him hanging.

Nurse Hayes and the Chinese hospital staff, who had been held under house arrest, were asked to claim his body. Miss Hayes noticed that his eyes were not bulging nor his tongue swollen, the usual features which would indicate hanging. But his upper body was a mass of bruises.

These devoted friends took his body to a cemetery. The Communists permitted no service and required the mourners to leave immediately after his body was lowered into the grave. But the Chinese could not be cowed. Defying the Communists, they returned and erected a shaft over his grave pointing heavenward. On the shaft they inscribed the Scripture which they felt described the motivation of his life:

"FOR TO ME TO LIVE IS CHRIST"

When Everly Hayes was released and returned home to tell the story, the head of the Southern Baptist Foreign Mission Board commented: "The Communists thought they were rid of him; instead they immortalized him." So true. *Bill Wallace of China*, by Jesse Fletcher (Broadman Press), had multiple printings. A film was made. Scores of young men and women committed their lives to missionary service. Said a Christian and Missionary Alliance missionary friend, "There have been and there will be many martyrs, but few can so glorify Him in death as Bill did."

The Fiery Trials of Chinese Believers

Chinese Christians and church leaders having close connections to President Chiang's Nationalist government were among the first targets of a Communist purge. Some were killed. Others managed to flee with Chiang's staunchest supporters to Taiwan.

One who escaped was Dr. Chen Wei-ping, who had been a Methodist pastor for over fifty years. In 1900 he was pastor of the First Methodist Church of Peking when the Boxers spilled their rivers of blood across north China. His church and home were burned, but he and his wife and young child escaped. His parents and brother and sister did not. Later Dr. Chen had been told the gruesome story of his family's murder. He had borne the memory for almost fifty years. Now, with the Communist takeover, he too was willing to die for Christ. But leaders of the defeated government begged, "Come with us. We need you more." He went to Taiwan and became Chief of Chaplains in the Nationalist Army. Later he became pastor of the Shih Ling Church which President and Madame Chiang regularly attended.

Many thousands of Christians stayed behind, telling departing missionaries and fleeing Chinese friends, "We ask only that you pray for us as we remain to face the storm."

The storm broke on Catholics more suddenly than Protestants. The Reds tried to induce the Catholic clergy to set up an independent Chinese Patriotic Church but met stiff resistance. A crackdown resulted, and hundreds of priests were imprisoned. Before 1952 about one hundred Chinese clergy died in jail. In 1952 over two hundred perished. By 1954 an additional four to five hundred priests had joined these martyrs. Not until 1958 was the puppet church established, and then it was denounced by the Pope. Most of the remaining opponents of the new church were put in prison.

The Marxist regime had more success with Chinese Protestants. In 1950 Chou En-lai persuaded a few leaders to draft "the Christian Manifesto," affirming loyalty to the government and opposition to "imperialism, feudalism, and bureaucratic capitalism." Chinese "volunteers" were then fighting in Korea. The anti-foreign spirit for past western aggressions remained strong. With support from liberal churchmen, some trained in liberal American seminaries, three hundred thousand Chinese Protestants signed the Manifesto.

The next tactic was the "Resist-America, Aid-Korea, Three-Self-Reform Movement" (self-support, self-government, and self-propagation), followed by the organization of a unified Chinese Christian Church with officers from Three-Self Committees. All denominational structures were dismantled. Services were allowed only in authorized church buildings at announced hours with a government monitor present. By 1958 only a dozen of two hundred churches in Shanghai were open; in Peking only four of sixty-five still held services.

From the beginning of the Red takeover there had been Christian resistance. In Manchuria a Christian leader protested indiscriminate killing. He was dragged into a People's Court and accused of numerous crimes against "the people." The judges ordered spectators to march by him, each to hit him with a club until he was beaten to death. But the people refused, declaring, "He's a good man."

Changing tactics, the judges promised that if he renounced Jesus he would be set free. "Which do you choose—Jesus Christ or Communism?" they demanded.

"Jesus! Jesus! Jesus!" he shouted back.

Then they took him to the river bank for execution. Along the way he sang, "Jesus Loves Me" and the Twenty-third Psalm set to Chinese music. He asked to pray, and they granted him permission to kneel briefly. When he stood up, he was shot in the back. But instead of falling on his face to grovel in the dust as victims usually do, he fell backwards, as if he were falling into the arms of Jesus. The entire community was reportedly stirred by his testimony.

In Shansi Province, scene of bloody Boxer massacres, many evangelists and pastors were martyred. In one instance, a preacher was tortured, then told he could go but dare not preach again.

"No, I cannot do that," he replied. "I cannot obey you."

Furious, the official shouted, "Then you must die, you miserable lout."

"I am not the one who is poor and miserable," the preacher replied calmly, and he began preaching to the man. He was shot without further delay.

There was widespread resistance to joining the puppet National Christian Church. This resistance was concentrated in the communal Jesus Family and the Little Flock house churches. Neither had direct connections with missionaries. Thousands of Chinese participants in the house churches of these groups were killed or imprisoned. Best known in the West for his books was Watchman Nee, leader of the Little Flock. He was imprisoned in 1952 and lived until June, 1972.

A deceitful calm came in 1957 when many political prisoners were released and Mao Tse-tung proclaimed as state policy, "Let all flowers bloom and all schools of thought contend." This was taken as an invitation to speak up. Some church leaders charged the Three-Self Movement with taking away their political rights. One churchman called the lack of personal freedom under the government "intolerable." The veteran evangelist Chia Yu-ming told theological students that the "mark of the beast" as revealed in Revelation was membership in the Communist Party. Another faculty member at this seminary displayed a poem that challenged atheism:

>I say, God is; you say No;
>Let's see who will suffer woe.
>You say, No God; I say you're wrong;
>We'll see who sings Salvation's Song.

The bloom faded. Most of those who had been released from prison when the deceitful invitation was announced were rounded up and put back in jail. One of these was Henry H. Lin, who had previously been arrested in 1957. Before that time he had been president of the Baptist University of Shanghai, succeeding Herman Liu, a martyr to the Japanese. President Lin languished less than two years in prison. According to a report, he was given a higher release when he died in a jail near Nanking early in 1960.

Too late the critics learned they had been tricked. The Communists now knew who the resisters were and began hauling them into court for crimes against the state.

In one city fifty-two pastors, evangelists and leading laymen were put on trial and pressured to make confessions. During the procedure, Communist supporters were invited to display their loyalty by slapping, pulling the hair and spitting on the accused. The inquisition continued for seven days and the last two nights. On September 7, 1958, one pastor collapsed and died. He was rolled up in a reed mat and dumped in a grave before his widow knew he was dead. When she asked permission to move the body to their home burial ground, the Communists jeered, "You Christians are going to heaven. Why do you worry about burial?" As a result of this pastor's death, seventeen of his co-defendants denounced Communist injustice and were immediately sentenced to long terms of hard labor under inhuman conditions.

Astute China observers believe that similar trials occurred all over China, leading to imprisonment for thousands of Christian leaders. Communist secrecy insures that the records will never be publicized.

But thousands more were absorbed into the Communist plan with little murmur. They came largely from the leadership of denominations included in the national union church (Methodists, United Church of Christ or Congregationalists, Presbyterians, and others). They had been conditioned for the Communist appeal by liberal theology professors who themselves were largely trained in the United States.

Protestant liberalism, deemphasizing and demythologizing miracles and biblical authority, introduced the powerful but crippling secularism into Chinese Christianity. Yale's late distinguished Professor in Missions and Oriental History, Kenneth S. Latourette, termed "the secularizing movements issuing from alleged Christendom and the essence of the Christian Gospel as seen in the apparent weakness of the incarnation and the cross" as the most important factor in the reverse suffered by Christianity in Communist China. More important than the association of China missions with western imperialism, Latourette said.

The Chinese Church Refuses to Die

What of Christianity today behind the bamboo curtain?

In recent years hard news of the state of Christianity in China has been scarce. There were a million baptized Protestants and around three million Catholics at the time of the Communist takeover. Journalists and other visitors report seeing only a few showcase churches still open and these are sparsely attended. Unauthorized meetings of three or more persons are illegal. The "president" of the Nanking Theological Seminary admitted in 1977 that he had had no students in five years.

Relatives outside the bamboo curtain occasionally get news of their loved ones. Franklin Liu, for example, a Baptist educator in Hongkong and the son of martyred Herman Liu, heard that his mother remained under house arrest in Peking, his brother was in a labor camp in Manchuria, and his sister was allowed to teach mathematics in Shanghai. That news was several years ago and their fate is now unknown.

But letters to the Far Eastern Broadcasting Company in Manila, stories from refugees trickling into Hongkong, and reports from Chinese allowed to visit relatives inside China suggest that cell churches are thriving in some areas. Among a population of thirty thousand in an area near the coast, three thousand believers are said to be meeting in small house churches. But sources for this report also say that plundering Red Guards during the height of the Cultural Revolution destroyed almost all Bibles in the district.

David Adeney, dean of OMF's Discipleship Training Centre in Singapore and a veteran China watcher, tells in *Christianity Today* (18 November 1977) of a Hongkong resident who visited his relatives and found almost all of them still professing Christians. Relatives told him many had been baptized in 1976 and numbers of young people were seeking Christ. These were being warned that the cost of commitment could be great. The times and places of house church meetings were constantly being changed to avoid a crackdown. Nevertheless, leaders continue to be arrested and sent to labor camps. At one meeting worshipers "strongly sensed the presence of the Spirit of God and the love of Christ." At the conclusion of the meeting, five visitors stood and announced they had been sent to make arrests. Now they too wanted to believe. They were then instructed to kneel and confess their sins and receive salvation in Christ.

Adeney tells of another Chinese Christian who came to Hongkong with his five-year-old daughter to visit his father. He had left his wife behind in an area where Christians feared to confess their faith. He recalled that he and his wife sometimes prayed together in bed, but had been afraid to tell their child for fear she would tell in kindergarten and bring trouble upon them.

Adeney further reports news of a powerful revival in one section of China. In this area five hundred Christian leaders associated with Watchman Nee were arrested. The newsbearer said that five of eleven who came from his village were sent to a remote spot from which only one returned. Three died of extreme cold and hard labor. One was shot because of his continued witness. But in 1976 revival swept the area and four to five thousand were baptized in secluded places.

What is the future for Christianity in earth's most populous nation (900 million) where more martyr blood has undoubtedly been shed than anywhere else in modern times? Perhaps the answer can be found in a charred page from the New Testament, recovered by a Christian after the Red Guards had burned his Bible. Standing out were these words: "Upon this rock I will build my church; and the gates of hell shall not prevail against it."

BY THEIR BLOOD
Christian Martyrs of the 20th Century
by James & Marti Hefley

Now! For the first time, a detailed, complete, and unabridged biography of Christian martyrs who were tried and tested, and who finally died for their faith in this so-called "civilized" 20th Century. *By Their Blood* is an extraordinary legacy of horror and death—and yet triumph and hope, amid the ashes of human defeat! Read *By Their Blood: Christian Martyrs of the 20th Century*. Only here will the best-selling authors, James and Marti Hefley, take you through Africa, Asia, the Americas, the Middle East, and Europe where violence and bloodshed—senseless crimes of hatred against Christian believers—are thoroughly documented and accurately reported. Sure to be a national best-seller, *By Their Blood* begins where *Foxe's Book of Martyrs* leaves off. Here is the total picture of which *China! Christian Martyrs of the 20th Century* is only an excerpt. Here is the complete story. It is a stirring and profound testimony of faith and courage at work—at the doorsteps of death.

**(This may very well be the
most important book you read all year!)**

------------------------------ ORDER NOW ------------------------------

Buy them at your local bookstore,
or use this handy coupon for ordering.

Mott Media P.O. Box 236 Milford, MI 48042

Yes! Please send me _____ copies of *By Their Blood* by James and Marti Hefley in cloth @ $9.95. Orders for less than 5 copies must include 60¢ for the first book and 25¢ for each additional copy to cover mailing and handling. Postage FREE for orders of 5 books or more. Check or money order only. Please include sales tax.

Name _____

Address _____

City _____

State _____ Zip _____

mott media

*We're meeting the need
of more people . . . through
inspirational books.*

_____ Books @ $9.95 Total $ _____

Shipping/Handling $ _____

Sales Tax $ _____

Total Cost $ _____

Please allow 4–6 weeks for delivery.